BUILDING BETTER BEHAVIOR

BHAWNA AGGARWAL "SONIA", BCBA

BUILDING BETTER BEHAVIOR

Copyright © 2025 by Bhawna Aggarwal (Sonia), All rights reserved.

No part of this publication may be reproduced, distributed, or transmitted in any form or by any means, including photocopying, recording, or other electronic or mechanical methods, without the prior written permission of the publisher, except in the case of brief quotations embodied in critical reviews and certain other non-commercial uses permitted by copyright law. For permission requests, write to the publisher at the email address below.

Published by: Cognifi Media House

Disclaimer:
The information contained in this book is intended for educational purposes only. While every effort has been made to ensure accuracy, the publisher and author assume no responsibility for errors or omissions, or for damages resulting from the use of the information contained herein. The techniques and strategies presented may not be suitable for every individual. Professional advice should be sought for specific situations.

I would like to dedicate this work to all parents and caretakers around the world, professionals and non-professionals, who are in the frontline of helping children to grow and develop – this incredibly difficult and challenging job. We salute your commitment, dedication, unconditional love and tireless efforts to help your children grow and develop. By this work, we acknowledge your strengths, your struggles, your successes, and most importantly, we are grateful for your continuous efforts in trying to make a better future for your children. In this regard, we do hope that the strategies suggested in this work will help you substitute your challenges with successes and rejoice in all the attempts and efforts that you are making. Your journey of being a parent is a great proof of how much love a parent can express and what an incredible potential every child possesses. So, thank you sincerely for being so amazing and remember, you are always the most important person for your child even when you face numerous challenges trying to be the best to your child. It is all for you, and we do hope that this work will provide you comfort, understanding and strategies on how to help your child as a parent.

Best Regards,
Bhawna Aggarwal "Sonia"
MS (Psychology), BCBA, IBA, LBA (Texas, North Carolina), RBA (Ontario)
Email: get2soniabcba@gmail.com
LinkedIn: https://www.linkedin.com/in/basonia/
Educational Blogs: get2sonia.medium.com

CONTENTS

Front Matter — v

Skill Acquisition — 1
   1 Foundations First — 2
   2 From Diagnosis to Therapy — 5
   3 Journey To ABA — 11
   4 Key ABA Teaching Strategies — 34
   5 Visual Supports — 51
   6 Structured Choice-Making — 61
   7 Teaching Complex Skills using shaping and chaining — 66
   8 Toilet Training — 76
   9 Behavioral Contracts — 86

Addressing Challenging Behaviors — 89
   10 Behavior: What & Why — 90
   11 Build an Effective Behavior Intervention Plan — 103
   12 Phases of Challenging Behavior — 116

Back Matter — 119
References — 120
About the Author — 122

Skill Acquisition

CHAPTER 1

Foundations First

When you're new to ABA (Applied Behavior Analysis), it can feel like learning a new language. Don't worry! Here are some common ABA terms explained in simple language to help you feel more confident when supporting a child.

BASIC TERMINOLOGY

Foundational ABA Concepts

- **Behavior** – Anything a person says or does.
- **Antecedent** – What happens *before* a behavior.
- **Consequence** – What happens *after* a behavior.
- **Reinforcement** – Reinforcement means giving a reward or something nice after a behavior so the person will do it again.
- **Punishment** – Punishment means giving a consequence or something unpleasant after a behavior so the person will do it less.
- **Positive Reinforcement** – Adding something good (e.g., praise, candy).
- **Negative Reinforcement** – Removing something unpleasant (e.g., loud noise).
- **Positive Punishment** – Adding something unpleasant (e.g., scolding).

- **Negative Punishment** – Taking away something the person likes (e.g., toy).
- **Extinction** – Stopping reinforcement to reduce a behavior.

* * *

Main Skill Types

- **Mand** – Asking for what you want (e.g., "juice").
- **Tact** – Labeling something (e.g., "dog" when you see a dog).
- **Echoic** – Repeating what someone says.
- **Intraverbal** – Answering or filling in (e.g., "Twinkle, twinkle, little…").
- **Listener Responding** – Doing something when someone tells you to (e.g., "clap your hands").
- **Imitation** – Copying actions or words.
- **Matching** – Putting the same things together.
- **Sorting** – Grouping by color, shape, etc.
- **Receptive Language** – Understanding what others say.
- **Expressive Language** – Saying or signing something.

* * *

Foundational Teaching Tools

- **Prompt** – Help to get the correct answer (e.g., hand-over-hand).
- **Prompt Fading** – Gradually removing help.
- **Error Correction** – Fixing a mistake by teaching the right answer.

- **Generalization** – Doing the skill in different places or with different people.
- **Maintenance** – Keeping the skill over time.
- **Shaping** – Teaching by rewarding small steps.
- **Chaining** – Breaking tasks into steps (like brushing teeth).
- **Discrete Trial Training (DTT)** – A structured way of teaching, with clear beginning and end.

* * *

Problem Challenging Behavior

- **Elopement** – Running away from a safe space.
- **SIB (Self-Injurious Behavior)** – Hurting oneself.
- **Aggression** – Hurting others (e.g., hitting, biting).
- **Tantrum** – Crying, yelling, falling to the floor.
- **Pica** – Eating things that aren't food.
- **Stereotype/Stereotypy** – Repeated movements or sounds (e.g., hand-flapping).
- **Noncompliance** – Not following directions.
- **Escape Behavior** – Trying to get away from something (e.g., work).
- **Attention-Seeking Behavior** – Acting out to get others to look or respond.
- **Automatic Behavior** – A behavior that feels good on its own (no outside reward).

Learning these ABA terms is important for building a strong foundation, so as you go through this book, it will be easier for you to understand each concept.

CHAPTER 2

From Diagnosis to Therapy

WHY EARLY INTERVENTION IS IMPORTANT

Early intervention is important because a child's brain is more flexible and adaptable during the early years of life, a concept known as **neuroplasticity**. Neuroplasticity refers to the brain's ability to change and form new connections in response to learning and experience. When therapy begins early, especially before the age of 5, the brain is more responsive to intervention, which can lead to faster progress in communication, social skills, behavior, and learning.

Starting therapy as soon as possible after diagnosis helps reduce the impact of developmental delays and increases the likelihood of long-term success. Early intervention can also improve the child's ability to function more independently and participate meaningfully in daily life.

What to Do If You Notice Developmental Delays in a Child

Let's jump into what to do if developmental delays or red flags are noticed in a child's growth. The first step is to contact a family doctor to discuss the concerns and request a developmental screening or a referral to a specialist.

Who is Eligible to Diagnose Your Child?

The professionals who can diagnose developmental concerns in a child include a pediatrician, developmental pediatrician, child psychologist, and child psychiatrist. This can change according to the country/state/province. When reading this book, keep in mind that your child's evaluation should always be conducted by a qualified professional in your area who can provide a thorough assessment and guidance.

Seeking Appropriate Therapies After an Autism Diagnosis

Once a child is diagnosed with autism, it's important to seek appropriate therapies based on their specific needs. The type of therapy chosen should be tailored to address the challenges identified in the diagnosis. The therapies may include ABA therapy, speech-language therapy (SLP), occupational therapy, physiotherapy, etc., depending on the child's needs.

WHY ABA (APPLIED BEHAVIOR ANALYSIS) IS CONSIDERED THE BEST THERAPY FOR CHILDREN WITH AUTISM

ABA (Applied Behavior Analysis) is widely regarded as one of the most effective therapies for children with autism, with substantial evidence supporting its effectiveness. Here are some key points based on research and findings that highlight why ABA is considered the best therapy for children with autism:

1. **Proven Effectiveness:** Research consistently demonstrates that ABA therapy leads to significant improvements in communication, social skills, and behavior for children with autism. A meta-analysis published in *The Journal of Autism and Developmental Disorders* (2014) found that children who received ABA therapy showed improvements in cognitive and adaptive skills.

2. **Early Intervention Success:** Studies show that children who begin ABA therapy at an early age tend to experience the greatest improvements. The *National Institutes of Health* (2019) reports that early intervention using ABA techniques can help children acquire essential skills and reduce challenging behaviors, leading to long-term benefits.
3. **Reduction in Problem Behaviors:** ABA therapy is highly effective in reducing challenging behaviors such as aggression, self-injury, and tantrums. By reinforcing positive behaviors and teaching alternative skills, children learn how to communicate their needs in more appropriate ways. This approach has been documented in multiple studies, including *Behavior Analysis in Practice* (2018), which found significant reductions in problem behaviors with ABA.
4. **Individualized Treatment:** One of the strengths of ABA therapy is its ability to be tailored to each child's unique needs. Behavior Analysts customize interventions based on individual assessments, ensuring that the therapy is both effective and relevant to the child's specific challenges and goals.
5. **Long-Term Benefits:** The impact of ABA therapy is not limited to the duration of treatment. Research indicates that the benefits of ABA can last long after therapy ends. A study published in *The Journal of Applied Behavior Analysis* (2020) showed that children who underwent ABA therapy continued to demonstrate improvement in functional skills and behavior even after therapy concluded.
6. **Endorsement by Leading Organizations**: ABA therapy is regulated by well-known states/provinces and organizations such as the *Behavior Analyst Certification Board (BACB)* in the USA and Canada and various professional associations. These organizations ensure that ABA therapists are trained and certified to provide effective and ethical treatment. ABA is recognized as the

gold standard in autism treatment and is widely recommended by healthcare providers and experts in the field of autism.

***

A PARENT'S GUIDE TO ABA THERAPY: WHAT TO EXPECT FROM PROFESSIONAL SERVICES

When you begin the ABA therapy journey, the first step is typically reaching out to an ABA center. The center will provide information about their services and ask you to complete some paperwork, including details about the child's diagnosis and any previous assessments. After this, a Board Certified Behavior Analyst (BCBA), along with a team that may include Registered Behavior Technicians (RBTs) or Assistant Behavior Analysts, will conduct an initial assessment. During this process, the BCBA uses evidence-based assessment tools such as the ABLLS, VB-MAPP, PEAK, etc., to evaluate the child's current skills and areas of need. They assess important areas like adaptive behavior, communication, social play, problem-solving, imitation skills, etc. The BCBA will also identify learning barriers such as problem behaviors, limited attention span, sensory sensitivities, social challenges, lack of motivation, etc. All of this information helps create an individualized treatment plan designed to help the child learn, grow, and succeed in daily life. A key part of the therapy process is parent coaching, where the BCBA teaches you how to apply ABA strategies at home to support the child during routines like playtime, mealtimes, transitions, etc. In this book, I'll share many of these practical strategies so parents can develop a strong understanding of ABA and confidently support the child's progress.

ABA therapy is an ongoing process where the child's progress is carefully monitored over time. The therapy team collects data during each session, and the BCBA regularly reviews this data to track the child's growth, assess what's working, and adjust any teaching methods as needed. If the child isn't meeting certain goals, the BCBA will make necessary changes to better support the child's success. They also stay alert to new challenges that may arise—such as shifts in motivation, changes in the environment, new behaviors, etc.—and update the plan to address these barriers. Every six months (or sooner, if needed), the BCBA completes a formal reassessment to evaluate the child's overall progress and update goals to match their developing skills. The goal is always to help the child continue growing, remove obstacles to learning, and ensure the treatment plan evolves to meet their changing needs.

* * *

THE KEY DIFFERENCES BETWEEN ABA AND IBI

Many people get confused between ABA and IBI because the terms sound similar, but they are a bit different (table 1). ABA (Applied Behavior Analysis) is a broad science that studies how people learn and behave. It uses various strategies to teach positive behaviors and reduce problem behaviors. ABA can be used with anyone—children, teens, or adults—and can take place at home, school, clinics, or in the community. It's not only for autism but for anyone who needs help with learning or behavior.

IBI (Intensive Behavioral Intervention) is a very focused, intensive form of ABA, mostly used with young children with autism. In IBI, children usually get many hours of therapy each week—often 20 to 40 hours. This therapy is very detailed and works on important skills like communication, play, self-care, social skills, and cognitive skills etc. Both ABA and IBI programs are carefully planned by a Behavior Analyst, with trained therapists teaching the child one-on-one.

Simply put, ABA is the big umbrella of behavior change techniques, and IBI is a special, intense type of ABA designed to give young children strong, early support. ABA therapy hours can be flexible, depending on the child's needs, while IBI is always intensive, with many hours per week to help children learn important skills faster.

Choosing between ABA and IBI depends on the child's individual needs, age, and the intensity of support required. Consulting with a qualified Behavior Analyst can help families decide which approach will be the most effective for their child's growth and development.

Aspect	ABA	IBI
What It Is	A broad method to teach positive behaviors and skills	A focused, intensive ABA program for young children with autism
Who It's For	People of all ages who need behavior support	Mainly young children diagnosed with autism
Therapy Time	Flexible; hours vary based on needs	Intensive; usually 20 to 40 hours per week
Areas of Focus	Wide range of skills and behaviors	Early skills like communication, social, and self-care
How It's Done	One-on-one or group sessions led by a BCBA	One-on-one therapy sessions led by a BCBA

Table 1: Difference between ABA and IBI

CHAPTER 3

Journey To ABA

PAIRING

Pairing is the very first step in ABA therapy. It means the therapist or technician spends time building a positive and trusting relationship with the child. They do this by playing games the child likes, offering favorite toys or treats, and creating a fun environment without asking too many questions or giving instructions right away. This helps the child feel comfortable and happy around the therapist. When pairing is done well, the child will enjoy spending time with the therapist and see learning as something fun.

<u>What You Can Do as a Parent</u>

As a parent, you can build this positive relationship by spending quality time with your child every day. Let them decide what they want to play and follow their lead without giving instructions or asking too many questions. Just enjoy the moment with them—whether you're playing with toys, reading, or being silly together. These fun, pressure-free times help your child feel happy, safe, and connected to you, which makes it easier for them to enjoy learning with you and following your lead.

INSTRUCTIONAL CONTROL

Instructional control happens after pairing is successful. It means the child willingly follows the therapist's instructions because they have learned that doing so leads to positive, fun, and rewarding experiences. Instructional control is built through trust, especially consistency, and by making learning enjoyable for the child. When the therapist gains instructional control, it becomes easier to teach new skills and help the child grow while enjoying the learning process together.

What You Can Do as a Parent

You can help the child learn to follow instructions by pairing regularly. If the child doesn't understand what you are asking, help them at first and gradually stop helping as they master the steps. If the child is struggling with a big or difficult task, break it down into smaller, easier steps. Once the child masters the easier steps, gradually make the tasks a bit harder. When the child listens and follows instructions, reward them immediately with praise, a smile, or something motivating. Be patient and consistent, and keep learning fun. Over time, the child will learn that following instructions leads to positive outcomes. Regular praise, smiles, and spending time together are key to maintaining instructional control.

* * *

EVERY CHILD CAN COMMUNICATE: EXPLORING SPEECH, PECS, AND AAC DEVICES

Communication is how the child shares their needs, thoughts, and feelings with others. Every child is different, and not all children use spoken words right away or in the same way. That's why we use many different methods to help children communicate effectively, depending on what works best for them. One of the simplest ways to start communication is through pointing and gestures. For example, when a child points at a toy, a snack, or a person, they are trying to tell you something without using words. Teaching the child to point or use simple gestures, like waving "hello" or shaking their head "no," gives them a way to express themselves and connect with others, even before they can speak.

Another popular method is the Picture Exchange Communication System (PECS). PECS uses pictures that represent objects, actions, or ideas. The child learns to pick up a picture and hand it to the other person to communicate what they want or need. For example, if the child is hungry, they might hand a picture of food. PECS helps children who find it hard to talk still communicate clearly and be understood. It gives the child a way to express their needs and wants and encourages interaction between the child and the people around them.

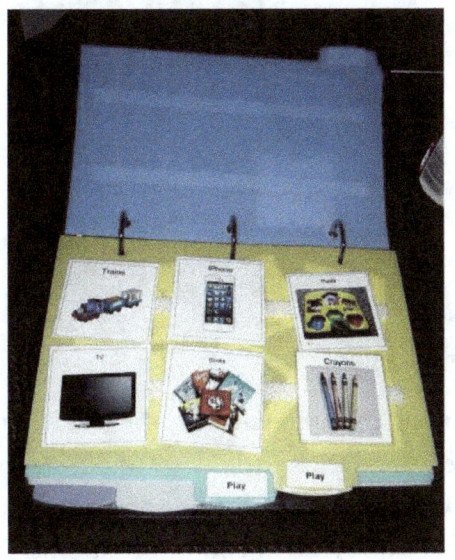

Image 1: Picture Exchange Communication System (PECS)

For some children, Augmentative and Alternative Communication (AAC) devices offer a high-tech way to communicate. AAC devices can be tablets, special computers, or buttons with pictures or symbols that the child can press to "speak" for them. These devices produce spoken words or phrases, giving children a voice even if they cannot speak clearly yet. AAC includes software programs like Proloquo2Go and GoTalk, which are customizable to match the child's abilities and needs. Using these different communication methods—pointing, PECS, AAC devices, and spoken language—helps the child express themselves, build relationships, and take part in daily life more fully.

Image 2: AAC Device

* * *

VERBAL OPERANTS

Verbal operants are the different ways the child communicates to get their needs met, share what they see or think, and interact with others. For example, when the child asks for something like "juice" because they are thirsty, that's one kind of communication called a mand. When they see a dog and say "dog," they are naming or labeling what they see, which is called a tact. The child also uses other kinds of communication when they answer questions or take part in a conversation, like saying "yes" when asked if they want to play; this is called an intraverbal. Sometimes the child may copy or repeat words they hear, which helps them learn new sounds and words, and this is called echoic behavior. Each type of communication serves a special purpose and helps the child connect with people around them. Teaching all these different ways to communicate helps the child build important skills for everyday life, making it easier for them to express themselves clearly and understand others better.

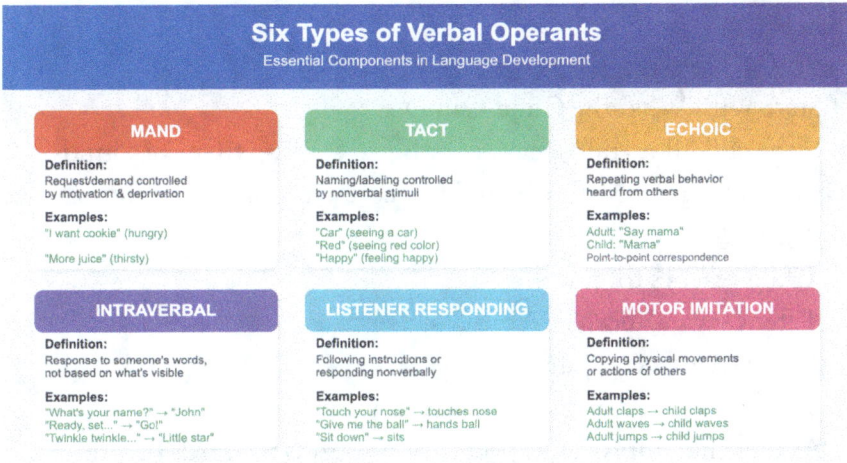

Image 3: Six types of verbal operants

Manding

What It Is

Manding means asking for what the child wants or needs. Children can do this in many ways—by using words, gestures, signs, pointing, or communication tools like PECS (Picture Exchange Communication System) or AAC (Augmentative and Alternative Communication) devices.

Why Is It Important?

When children learn to ask for things, they can communicate their needs to others. This helps reduce frustration for both the child and those around them. Manding is one of the most important early communication skills. Teaching it helps the child learn new words and interact better with others.

How Parents Can Help

Parents can help by paying attention to what the child enjoys and creating more opportunities for them to ask for those things. The more chances the child has to practice, the stronger their communication skills will become. Be patient, gently guide them, and celebrate every small success.

Tips & Examples for Parents

Start With What the Child Can Do

If the child does not speak yet or is just starting to make sounds, help them learn to ask for things by encouraging any effort they make.

Example

Child reaches for juice.

Parent says, "Juice! Say 'juice.'"

Child tries to say "juh."

Parent says, "Great try! Here's your juice!"

As the child improves, expect clearer sounds or words before giving the item. This step-by-step method is called shaping.

How to shape the word "juice":

Step 1: When the child makes any sound, give the juice. At this stage, even small sounds or mouth movements count as communication attempts.

Step 2: Once the child has mastered making sounds, give juice only when the sound is closer to "juice," such as "juh" or "jui"—not for any random sound.

Step 3: After the child has mastered saying "juh" or "jui," give juice only when the child clearly says "juh."

Step 4: Once the child has mastered saying "juh," give juice only when the child attempts the full word "juice."

Step 5 (advanced): When the child has mastered saying "juice," encourage expanding to a short phrase like "want juice." Give juice after the full phrase is spoken.

If the Child Uses Single Word
Encourage the child to move from single words to simple phrases to improve clarity and communication skills.
Example
Child says: "Cookie."
Parent says: "Nice asking! Can you say 'want cookie'?"
Child tries: "Want cookie."
Parent: "That's it! Here you go."

Child says: "Milk."
Parent says: "Say 'more milk'."
Child tries: "More milk."
Parent: "Perfect! Here's your milk."
With each step, once the child has mastered it, model the next level of speech and provide a reward only when they attempt or try that next level. This approach helps the child progress in their communication skills.

If the Child Uses PECS or an AAC Device
If the child uses pictures or a communication device, encourage them to use PECS or the device before giving them what they want. This helps the child learn to request appropriately and strengthens their communication skills.
Example
Child looks at the items.
Parent presents the PECS book during the initial stage.
Child hands over or taps the picture for "juice."
Parent says, "Juice? Great asking!" (Then gives the juice.)
How to Teach:

Start by giving the child the PECS book or AAC device and patiently wait for them to respond. If the child isn't sure what to do, gently help guide their hand to the picture or button. As soon as they make the attempt, immediately reward them with the item they asked for. Practice this often during snacks, play, or daily activities. Slowly lessen help so the child can learn to do it on their own.

Creating opportunities is an important way to help the child practice asking for things they want or need. This means setting up small situations where the child has to request help or an item to get what they want. For example, place favorite toys or snacks on a high shelf where the child can see them but cannot reach them easily. Keep toys inside a transparent box with the lid closed, so the child needs to ask for help to open it. Offer juice without a straw and wait for the child to ask for one. You can also partially open a door and wait for the child to ask to open it fully. Giving the child a puzzle with one piece missing and waiting for them to ask for that piece is another way to create a request opportunity. During playtime, you might hold back a favorite toy and wait for the child to ask before giving it. These simple strategies provide more opportunities for the child to practice communication naturally while keeping motivation high.

Echoics (Imitation of Sounds and Words)

<u>What It Is</u>
Echoics are when a child repeats what they hear—sounds, words, or short phrases—immediately after someone else says them. For example, if you say "ball" and the child repeats "ball," that's an echoic response. It's one of the earliest and most important steps in learning to talk. Echoics help children learn how to form sounds, produce words, and eventually speak independently.

<u>Why It's Important</u>

Echoics are essential for developing verbal language. When children repeat what they hear, they are strengthening their ability to speak, use their voice, and shape clear sounds. This imitation process builds the foundation for more advanced communication, including labeling (tacting), requesting (manding), and conversational exchanges (intraverbals). For children with limited speech, working on echoics can be the first big step toward using words to communicate.

How Parents Can Help

Parents can support the child's echoic skills by modeling words clearly and encouraging them to repeat after them. Use short, simple words at first, and celebrate any attempt—whether it's the full word or just part of it.

Tips & Examples for Parents

Start with Easy Sounds and Words: Begin with simple, motivating words—especially names of favorite toys, foods, or family members. Say the word clearly and invite the child to repeat it

Example:
Parent: "Juice. Say 'juice.'
Child: "Juh.
Parent: "Great job trying! Juice!"

Even if the child only says part of the word, reinforce it warmly. The goal is to shape the full word over time.

Use Fun and Repetition: Make imitation fun by turning it into a game. Use silly sounds, animal noises, or short songs to encourage echoing.

Example:
Parent: "Moo! Say 'moo.'"
Child: "Moo!"
Parent: "That's right! Cows say moo!"

Use sound play with animals, vehicles (vroom, beep), or common objects (pop, splash, yum) to make it enjoyable.

Shape Longer Responses: Once the child can echo single words, begin encouraging them to repeat two- or three-word phrases.

Example
Parent: "Want cookie. Say 'want cookie.'"
Child: "Want cookie."
Parent: "Great job copying me—'want cookie!'

We gradually increase the level, always starting at the child's current skill. Once they have mastered it, move gradually to the next, more advanced level.

Tacting (Labeling)

What It Is

Tacting is when a child labels or names things they see, hear, feel, taste, or smell. It's how a child might say "dog" when they see a dog, "blue" when they see a blue crayon, or "music" when they hear a song. Tacting helps children describe the world around them using words.

Tacts can include objects, people, animals, colors, sounds, actions, places, emotions, or anything else they experience. For example, saying "apple," "mommy," "train," or "dog" are all examples of tacting.

Why It's Important

Tacting plays a big role in helping children develop communication, social, and cognitive skills. When a child learns to tact, they are building vocabulary, making connections to the world around them, and learning how to share what they notice with others. It allows them to express thoughts, observations, and feelings. When children label what they see or hear, they become more aware of their environment. This awareness supports later language development, such as describing events, answering questions, and engaging in conversation.

How Parents Can Help

Parents can support tacting at home by labeling things in the child's environment and encouraging them to do the same. Use simple, natural language and look for opportunities throughout the day to model tacts—during meals, play, bath time, car rides, or family walks.

Tips & Examples for Parents

Start with One Word: If the child is just beginning to talk, focus on teaching them to label familiar items using single words. You can point to an object and say the word, encouraging the child to imitate.

Example:

Parent: (Pointing to the apple) "Say 'Apple.'"

Child: "Apple"

Parent: "Yes! That's right. Apple!"

Use toys, food, clothes, animals, and household items to make it fun and meaningful.

Expand to Two-Word Phrases: Once the child is comfortable labeling with one word, you can begin expanding their language by adding a descriptive word.

Example:

Child: Sees a ball and says, "Ball."

Parent: "Yes, that's a ball. It's a red ball! Say 'red ball.'"

Child: "Red ball"

Parent: "Great job saying 'red ball'!"

Over time, this helps the child notice colors, sizes, shapes, and other qualities of objects.

Move Toward Full Sentences: If the child is using two-word labels, you can guide them toward full sentences to help develop more expressive language.

Example:

Child: Sees a dog and says, "Brown dog."

Parent: "That's right! It's a brown dog. Say 'It's a brown dog.'"

Child: "It's a brown dog."

Parent: "Wow! You said the whole sentence: 'It's a brown dog.'"

You can also encourage labeling of actions:

Child: Sees people eating.

Parent: "They are eating. Say 'They are eating.'"

Child: "They are eating."

Parent: "Great job! You said it correctly! They are eating."

Intraverbals (Conversational Language)

What It Is

Intraverbals are words or phrases a child says in response to someone else's words. These are not based on things the child can see, hear, or touch in the moment—they're based on what the child knows or remembers. For example, if someone says, "What do you eat for breakfast?" and the child says, "Eggs," that's an intraverbal. Another example is when someone says, "Twinkle, twinkle, little..." and the child finishes with "star." Intraverbals are a big part of how we have conversations. They allow a child to respond to questions, participate in songs, fill in blanks, and eventually have back-and-forth exchanges with others.

Why It's Important

Intraverbals are key to helping children engage in social conversations, answer questions, and express ideas that aren't directly tied to what's in front of them. These skills build memory, language flexibility, and the ability to talk about past events, future plans, or things they imagine. Strengthening intraverbals helps children develop conversation skills and improves their ability to share thoughts and information with others. Intraverbals form the foundation for storytelling, classroom participation, and everyday interactions like answering "How was your day?" or "What do you want to do next?"

How Parents Can Help

Parents can build intraverbal skills at home by asking simple, predictable questions and encouraging the child to respond. Use songs, fill-in-the-blank games, or daily routines to practice. Be playful, use repetition, and celebrate all responses—even partial ones.

Tips & Examples for Parents

Start with Fill-in-the-Blank: Use simple phrases the child hears often, such as songs, books, or daily routines. Pause and let them fill in the missing word.

Example:
Parent: "Ready, set..."
Child: "Go!"

Parent: "Yes! Go!"

Parent: "Twinkle, twinkle little..."
Child: "Star."
Parent: "That's right! Star!"

Use songs, rhymes, and predictable routines to create lots of fun opportunities to practice.

Ask Simple WH- Questions: Start with easy, everyday questions the child can answer from experience. If they don't answer right away, say the answer and encourage them to repeat it.

Example:
Parent: "What do you wear on your feet?"
Child: "Shoes."
Parent: "Great job saying 'shoes'!"

Parent: "What color is the sun?"
Child: "Yellow."
Parent: "Good job! The sun is yellow."

Over time, parents can ask more open-ended questions, like:
"What do you eat for lunch?"
"What do you see at the zoo?"
"What do you do when you're tired?"

These questions help the child think, remember, and express ideas.

Expand to Conversation: Once the child can answer simple questions, begin teaching back-and-forth conversation skills. Start with short exchanges and build up.

Example:
Parent: "How are you?"
Child: "Good."
Parent: "I'm good too. What did you do today?"
Child: "Played.

At first, parents might model the full answer and have the child repeat

Parent: "Say, 'I played with blocks.'"
Child: "I played with blocks."
Parent: "Awesome! That's a great sentence."
Eventually, the child will begin responding more independently, using their own words and ideas.

Listener Responding (Understanding Words and Following Directions)

What It Is

Listener responding, also known as receptive language, is when a child understands and responds to what someone else says. It involves following instructions such as "Give me the ball," "Touch your nose," or "Point to the dog." Listener responding reflects the ability to hear a word or phrase and respond appropriately, even without speaking.

Skills in listener responding include following simple one-step directions, identifying objects, people, body parts, actions, or pictures when asked, and responding to everyday instructions.

Why It's Important

Understanding language is just as critical as using words. Strong listener responding skills help children make sense of verbal cues and instructions, which in turn support their ability to follow daily routines, engage in play and social interactions, and participate in school or group activities. These skills also lay the foundation for building expressive language, since understanding words is a prerequisite to using them effectively.

How Parents Can Help

You can promote listener responding at home by giving clear, simple instructions during everyday routines. Start with familiar items or actions and use gestures or modeling as needed. Celebrate successes, even if the child requires some assistance at first.

Tips & Examples for Parents

Start with Objects the Child Likes: Use toys, snacks, or familiar items. Place two or more items in front of the child and request one.

Example

Parent: (Places a ball and a car on the table) "Give me the ball."
Child: Picks up the ball and hands it to the parent.
Parent: "Nice job! You gave me the ball!"

If the child does not respond, gently prompt by pointing or guiding their hand, then praise when successful.

Use Body Parts and Simple Actions: Practice Body Parts and Simple Actions. Teach identification of body parts or following one-step movement directions.

Example

Parent: "Touch your nose."
Child: Touches nose
Parent: "That's right! Nose!"

Other examples:
"Clap your hands."
"Stand up."
"Wave bye-bye."

These activities build listening and comprehension skills in a playful way.

Try Picture Identification: Use picture books, flashcards, or printed images of familiar items. Ask the child to point to or give the picture you name.

Example:

Parent: "Where's the apple?"
Child: Points to the apple.
Parent: "Yes! That's the apple!"

Gradually increase difficulty by:

Adding more pictures

Mixing categories (animals, food, toys

Asking about colors or actions

Two-Step and Multi-Step Directions: Once the child reliably follows one-step instructions, progress to two-step directions to enhance memory and attention.

Examples:

Two-step: "Pick up your shoes and bring them to me."

Three-step: "Go to your room, get your book, and sit on the couch."

Four-step: "Take your backpack, put it by the door, take off your shoes, and wash your hands."

Give each instruction clearly and slowly. If the child makes an error or cannot follow the instruction, provide prompts such as physical guidance, gestures, modeling, etc. Praise the child for completing each step. This step-by-step progression strengthens listening skills and prepares the child for real-life tasks and classroom routines

Imitation (Learning by Copying Others)

What It Is

Imitation is when a child copies what someone else does. It could be copying actions like clapping hands, banging on a drum, waving, jumping, or even sticking out their tongue. In ABA, imitation is one of the earliest skills we teach because it helps children learn new actions, sounds, words, and social behaviors by watching others. Imitation includes both motor imitation (copying physical actions) and vocal imitation (echoics), but here we'll focus on motor imitation—copying actions with or without objects. We discussed echoics earlier as repeating sounds and words.

Why It's Important

Imitation is a building block for learning. Children who can imitate are more likely to learn through observation and repetition. Imitation supports the development of communication, social interaction, self-help skills, and play. When a child learns to copy others, they are not only learning new skills—they are also joining in shared activities and building stronger connections with those around them.

How Parents Can Help

You can help your child learn imitation by turning it into a fun game. Use clear, simple actions and encourage your child to "do what you do." Choose actions your child already enjoys, like clapping, stomping, or waving. Praise every attempt, even if it's not perfect.

Tips & Examples for Parents

Start with No-Object Imitation: Use simple body movements that are easy to see and copy.

Example:
Parent: (Claps hands) "Do this!"
Child: Claps hands.
Parent: "Yay! You copied me!"
Other easy imitation actions
 Stomp feet
 Tap head
 Raise arms
 Stick out tongue

If the child doesn't respond, model the action again or gently guide them while saying, "Do this."

Move to Object Imitation: Once your child can copy movements without objects, try using simple items like blocks, spoons, or toy drums.

Example:
Parent: (Bangs a spoon on the table) "Do this!"
Child: Bangs spoon.
Parent: "Great job copying!"
Other ideas:
 Stack a block
 Roll a ball

Shake a rattle

Push a toy car

Use Play and Songs: Songs with motions are a great way to encourage imitation in a fun and engaging way.

Example:

Parent: "If you're happy and you know it, clap your hands…" (Parent claps hands)

Child: Claps hands.

Parent: "Yes! You clapped just like me!"

Use familiar songs like "Wheels on the Bus," "Head, Shoulders, Knees and Toes," or "Itsy Bitsy Spider" to practice copying gestures.

***

TWO KEY TEACHING METHODS IN ABA: DTT VS. NET

In ABA therapy, there are many effective ways to help children learn new skills. Two of the most widely used and research-supported strategies are Discrete Trial Training (DTT) and Natural Environment Teaching (NET). Both are highly effective, but they differ in how and where teaching occurs. Understanding the strengths of each approach helps parents support their child's learning in both structured settings and everyday routines.

What Is Discrete Trial Training (DTT)

DTT is a structured teaching method that breaks skills into small, manageable steps. Each learning opportunity—called a *trial*—follows a consistent three-part sequence:

- The adult gives a specific instruction

- The child responds
- The adult provides immediate feedback (praise, reward, or correction)

DTT is typically done in a quiet, low-distraction setting—like a therapy room or table workspace—to help the child stay focused.

Example:
Therapist: "Touch your head."
Child: Touches head.
Therapist: "Great job! You touched your head!"

If the child gives an incorrect response, the adult may use a prompt or model the correct behavior, then offer another chance to try. Through Discrete Trial Training (DTT), we can teach a wide variety of skills across all developmental domains—such as adaptive behavior, cognitive functioning, receptive and expressive communication, academic readiness, social interaction, and more. Its repetitive structure and clear format make it especially effective for teaching new concepts and tracking progress over time. We will discuss some of the teaching strategies used in DTT in the next chapter, *Key ABA Teaching Strategies*.

What Is Natural Environment Teaching (NET)?

NET is a more flexible, play-based teaching method that occurs within the child's natural daily environment. Instead of working at a table with structured tasks, learning happens during real-life activities—such as playing, eating, getting dressed, or going to the park. The adult follows the child's lead and uses their interests to create meaningful teaching moments.

Example
Imagine the child loves playing with bubbles. The therapist holds the bubble container but does not open it yet. The child looks at the bubbles or reaches out for them.

Therapist: holds the bubbles and waits for the child to initiate

Child: looks at the bubbles or reaches toward them but does not say anything.

Therapist: waits for the child to ask, or prompts, "What do you want?" if needed.

Child: does not initiate.

Therapist: gently prompts the child by saying, "Say 'bubbles.'"

Child: says "bubbles."

Therapist: immediately blows bubbles and says, "Yes! Bubbles!" while reinforcing the correct mand or request.

NET makes learning fun, engaging, and natural. It encourages children to use their skills in different settings, with different people, and in more spontaneous ways—helping them generalize what they've learned. Unlike DTT, which is highly structured, NET takes advantage of daily routines, making learning feel like a natural part of life.

Just like DTT, NET can be used to teach skills across all developmental domains—including adaptive routines, communication, play, cognitive abilities, and academic concepts. Because NET is child-led and interest-based, motivation is often higher, and the learning experience becomes more meaningful. It also gives parents an easy and practical way to teach through everyday interactions without needing formal materials or time blocks.

<u>Teaching All Verbal Operants Through NET</u>

Some parents may wonder how to teach all areas of communication—especially the verbal operants—within NET sessions.

With a little creativity and consistency, NET can be used to teach all major verbal operants in meaningful, real-world contexts:

<u>Teaching Verbal Operants Through Pretend Kitchen Play</u>

In this example, we are using a kitchen set, but these strategies can be applied to any Natural Environment Teaching (NET) activity. Here's how different verbal operants can be taught during play:

Manding (Requesting): Set up situations where the child needs to request items. For example, if the child wants a spoon for their plate or is looking for a plastic knife to cut vegetables, wait for them to request it verbally or with a gesture. It depends on what communication level they are at and what your goals for teaching are. Prompt if needed, then give the item right away.

Tacting (Labeling): Hold an item like a spatula or cup and ask, "What is this?" The child can respond by labeling it (e.g., "spatula"). This helps them learn to name objects around them.

Intraverbals (Conversational Language): Ask questions like "What do you eat in the morning?" or "Where can you find a spoon?" These questions don't rely on what the child sees, so they help build conversation skills and memory.

Echoics (Repeating): Say a word like " Cookie" and ask the child to repeat it. This helps with learning new vocabulary.

Listener Responding (Following Instructions): Give simple directions like "Show me the fork" or "Give me the spoon." The child learns to listen and respond correctly to verbal instructions.

Imitation (Copying): Model actions like stirring with a spoon or pouring pretend tea. Say "Do this," and encourage the child to copy your actions. Imitating movements helps them to later copy others' actions, and they can learn many skills without being directly taught by therapists or parents.

To support you, I've included helpful datasheets that show how each of these verbal operants can be naturally taught during NET sessions. These real-life examples will guide you in turning play, routines, and daily moments into powerful learning opportunities that strengthen the child's communication and independence.

Natural Environment Teaching (NET) Plan – Kitchen Set Example

Child Name: Kane (Hypothetical Name)		
Activity Name: Kitchen Set		**Material Required:** Kitchen Set
Manding aka requesting (Asking for items/actions) **Example:** Hold up a toy spoon but don't give it right away. Encourage the child to ask by saying, "I want the spoon" or pointing to it.	**Listener Responding (Following instructions)** **Example:** Say, "Put the cup on the plate" or "Stir the soup" and see if the child follows the direction.	**Echoing Sounds (Repeating sounds/words)** **Example:** Say, "Say 'yum yum!'" or "Say 'stir stir!'" while pretending to cook and encourage the child to repeat.
Motor Imitation (Copying movements) **Example:** Stir in a pretend pot and say, "Do this" while showing the motion. Have the child copy you.	**Tact (Naming things)** **Example:** Point to a pretend apple and ask, "What is this?" to encourage the child to name it.	**Intraverbal (Answering without seeing the answer)** **Example:** Ask, "What do we use to drink?" (Expected response: "Cup"). Or "What do we put in a pan?" (Expected response: "Food")

Natural Environment Teaching Example

Image 4: NET Data Sheet Sample - Example

Natural Environment Teaching (NET) Plan

Child Name:		
Activity Name:		Material Required:
Manding aka requesting (Asking for items/actions)	Listener Responding (Following instructions)	Echoing Sounds (Repeating sounds/words)
Motor Imitation (Copying movements)	Tact (Naming things)	Intraverbal (Answering without seeing the answer)

Image 5: NET Data Sheet Sample - Blank for parents to reuse

CHAPTER 4

Key ABA Teaching Strategies

Let's discuss some important strategies commonly used in Applied Behavior Analysis (ABA). These strategies are designed to help children learn new skills and build independence. They also support behavior reduction and encourage the development of positive behaviors.

UNDERSTANDING REINFORCEMENT

Reinforcement is a key principle in ABA and one of the most effective ways to teach and encourage positive behavior. Simply put, reinforcement means rewarding a behavior to make it more likely to happen again.

Think of it like this: when something good happens right after the child does something, they'll want to do it again. That "something good" is the reinforcer.

Reinforcement can come in many forms—anything a child enjoys, wants, or finds motivating. This could include:

- Social: Praise like "Great job!" or a high five
- Tangible: A favorite toy, snack, or sticker
- Activity-based: Extra time to play a game or watch a show
- Sensory: Access to music, lights, or bubbles

BUILDING BETTER BEHAVIOR — 35

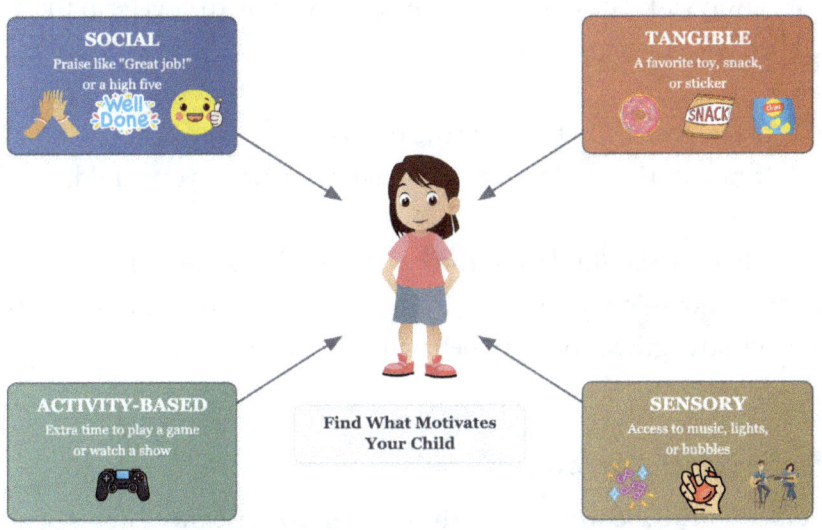

Image 1: Types of reinforcements

The first step in using reinforcement is discovering what motivates the child. What excites them? What do they enjoy or look forward to? It's important to remember that a reinforcer isn't just something the child likes—it's something that actually increases the behavior you want to see. We might think a toy, snack, or praise is a reinforcer because the child enjoys it—but if giving that item doesn't lead to more of the desired behavior, then it's not truly acting as a reinforcer.

Note: A reinforcer is only a reinforcer if it causes a behavior to happen more often.

Example:

If the child likes bubbles and you tell them they will get bubbles after cleaning up their toys—but they still don't clean up—then bubbles might not be an effective reinforcer for that behavior. The child may like bubbles, but simply liking something isn't enough—it has to bring change. We call something a reinforcer only if the child engages in the desired behavior to get the reward.

We always ask one question: Is the child willing to engage in the desired behavior to get the reward?

- If yes, great! You found a true reinforcer.
- If no, it's time to reassess what really motivates your child.

So when we say "find a reinforcer," we don't just mean something the child enjoys—we mean something they'll work for, and something that truly strengthens positive behavior over time.

Reinforcement Strategies

Once you've identified what the child enjoys, use those items or activities as reinforcers. Always pair reinforcement with specific verbal praise to make it more effective and promote natural learning. This also helps you gradually shift from tangible rewards (like snacks or toys) to social reinforcers (like praise), which are easier to maintain in everyday life. For Example, "I saw you picked up all your toys,Great work!" Specific praise clearly tells the child what they did well

Please remember that planning and consistency are key for reinforcement to work, it must be used consistently. If a child doesn't regularly receive reinforcement for a certain behavior, they may not learn the connection between the action and the reward.

<u>Example:</u> If you say the child will earn a sticker for cleaning their room, make sure to give the sticker each time they complete the task. This helps the child clearly understand the connection between cleaning the room and earning the reward. If the sticker is given only sometimes, or you forget to follow through, the child may become confused or less motivated to keep cleaning the room.

Immediacy Matters

The timing of reinforcement is just as important as the reward itself. The closer the reinforcement is delivered to the behavior, the stronger the association. If the child helps set the table, give reward immediately—not 30 minutes later. Delayed reinforcement weakens the connection between the behavior and the outcome, making it less likely the behavior will happen again.

How We Fade Reinforcement Over Time

When teaching a new skill—like cleaning up toys—we start by reinforcing the behavior every single time the child does it correctly. This helps them learn what's expected and feel motivated to do it again. For Example, You're teaching the child to clean up their toys. Every time they put the toys away, you give them a Skittle and say, "Great job cleaning up your toys!" At this stage, you're reinforcing every time to help them learn the new skill.

What Happens When the Skill Is Mastered?

Once the child has mastered and is showing the desired behavior consistently for a few days, such as cleaning up toys, it's time to fade the reinforcement. That means you don't give the Skittle every single time anymore. Instead, you might give it every 2 to 3 times they clean up, or even randomly.

<u>Example:</u>
The child cleans up, and you say:
"You cleaned up again—awesome!"
Then give a Skittle every second or third time.
This keeps them motivated but also teaches that they don't need a treat every time to keep doing the right thing.

Eventually...

As the child keeps succeeding, you can fade the Skittles completely and rely on social praise like:

"You're such a big helper!" or

"I'm so proud of you for cleaning up."

This way, the behavior continues with natural rewards—like feeling good or being praised by others—which are easier to maintain in daily life.

Reinforcement Is Not a Bribe—It's a Teaching Strategy

It's natural for parents to feel unsure when using rewards to shape behavior. You might wonder, *"Am I bribing my child?"* But there is an important difference between bribing and reinforcing behavior.

A bribe is given to stop a problem behavior that is already happening, while reinforcement teaches positive behavior and helps the child understand what is expected. Bribery may stop behavior in the short term but often strengthens the wrong behaviors in the long run. Reinforcement, on the other hand, strengthens positive behavior and encourages lasting change.

Think of reinforcement like a paycheck. Adults work first, then get rewarded. It's not a bribe—it's motivation. Children learn in the same way: So don't worry—you're not bribing the child. You're building a foundation for lifelong learning and behavior through clear, consistent, and positive reinforcement.

<u>Example:</u>

"If you stop screaming, I'll give you candy."

This teaches the child that misbehavior leads to rewards.

Reinforcement, on the other hand, is planned and proactive.

You decide in advance what behavior you want to encourage—like cleaning up toys or using kind words—and then reward the child after they do it.

PUNISHMENT

In behavior support—especially in ABA—punishment is not the first or preferred choice for managing behavior. While it may stop unwanted behavior in the short term, it often comes with negative side effects and fails to teach the child what to do instead. Promoting and reinforcing desired behavior helps children grow confidence, supports skill development, and encourages lasting positive change.

What Is Punishment?

Punishment means doing something after a behavior that makes it less likely to happen again. This could include scolding, removing privileges, or giving harsh consequences.

Image 2: Child is being scolded (Punishment)

Why We Avoid Punishment

It Doesn't Teach the Right Behavior: Punishment tells a child what *not* to do but doesn't show them what *to* do instead. For *Exam-*

ple: If you say, "Stop kicking!" when the child wants something but don't teach them how to ask appropriately, they won't learn a better way to communicate their needs.

It Can Lead to Escape or Avoidance: Children may try to avoid tasks or situations instead of learning from them. They might avoid the adult, shut down, or run away from the activity rather than build skills.

It Can Make Behavior Worse: Some children may respond to punishment with even more challenging behavior. They might throw tantrums, cry, refuse to listen, or become more upset and harder to calm down.

It Often Requires More Intensity Over Time: If a punishment works at first, it may need to become stronger over time to remain effective—leading to harsher and more unfair consequences.

It Reduces Motivation to Try: If children feel like they're always "in trouble," they may stop trying, withdraw, or feel discouraged about learning new skills.

***

PREFERENCE ASSESSMENT: FINDING WHAT MOTIVATES THE CHILD TO LEARN AND SUCCEED

What Is a Preference Assessment?

A preference assessment is a way to find out what items, activities, or rewards the child likes the most. This helps identify what motivates the child, so those things can be used as reinforcers during teaching and learning. Since every child is different, and their likes may change over time, conducting preference assessments regularly ensures that the most effective motivators are always being used.

<u>Why Is Preference Assessment Important?</u>

Using a reinforcer that the child enjoys makes it more likely they will want to learn, participate, and repeat positive behaviors. If you use something the child doesn't care about, it won't encourage the behavior. Preference assessments help make teaching more fun and effective by focusing on what truly interests the child.

How to Conduct a Preference Assessment

Before using reinforcement effectively, it's essential to find out what the child finds motivating. This process is called a preference assessment, and it involves observing or testing different items and activities to determine what the child prefers.

1. Free Operant Observation: Allow the child to freely access a variety of toys or activities. Observe which items they choose and how long they engage with each. This gives natural insight into their preferences.
2. Paired Choice Assessment: Offer two items at once and let the child choose. Rotate combinations and track which items are selected most often to identify stronger reinforcers.
3. Multiple Stimulus Without Replacement (MSWO): Present several items at once. After the child selects one, remove it and offer the rest again. The order of selection helps determine preference rankings.

Note: Make sure the child is not already holding a toy or item before starting, as it may affect their choices.

PROMPTING: DIFFERENT WAYS TO HELP WHEN THE CHILD DOESN'T KNOW A SKILL OR MAKES AN ERROR

What Is a Prompting?

Prompting is a teaching strategy used to help children learn new skills by providing guidance that increases the chance of a correct response. A prompt can be anything that supports the child—such as a verbal instruction, gesture, model, or physical assistance. The goal is to guide the child toward the correct response and prevent repeated errors.

Prompts are especially helpful when a child is learning something new, feels unsure about what to do, or makes errors after learning skills they have not practiced enough. Allowing a child to make multiple errors in the hope of speeding up independence can actually lead to frustration and slower learning. It is believed that if a child repeatedly makes errors, they may learn those errors, which can be difficult to correct later.

Prompting helps the child experience success and build confidence during learning. As the child becomes more independent, prompts are gradually reduced—a process called "fading." When a child is unsure what to do while learning a new skill, or makes an error after acquiring a skill but not practicing it enough, providing a prompt immediately helps guide them to the correct response. Reinforcing the correct response after prompting encourages learning the right behavior instead of repeating errors.

<u>Why Use Prompts?</u>
Prompts are used to:

- Help a child perform a skill they have not yet learned independently.
- Prevent repeated errors during the learning process.

- Build confidence by ensuring early success.
- Guide the child toward the correct behavior so they can receive reinforcement.

Prompting is not meant to be permanent—it's a short-term support to help the child learn the correct behavior until they no longer need help.

<u>Types of Prompts</u>
(*Arranged from most to least supportive—also called the "prompting hierarchy"*)

Full Physical Prompt
The adult physically guides the child's entire movement to complete a task.
Example: Hand-over-hand support to place a block into a shape sorter.

Partial Physical Prompt
A lighter touch or partial assistance.
Example: Gently nudging the child's elbow to guide their hand.

Model Prompt
Demonstrating the desired behavior or response.
Example: The adult says, "Wave bye-bye," and models the wave.

Gesture Prompt
Using gestures like pointing or motioning toward the correct choice.
Example: Pointing to the sink when asking the child to wash their hands.

Verbal Prompt
Using spoken words to help the child respond correctly, which could be the full answer, part of the answer, or a hint or clue.
Example: When showing a picture of a dog, and the child does not recognize the image, you will say, "Say 'dog.'"

Visual Prompt
Providing visual aids such as pictures, icons, written words, or visual schedules.

Example: A picture of a toothbrush to remind the child to brush their teeth.

Textual Prompt

Presenting written words or sentences to guide the child.

Example: You ask, "What is your address?" and the child doesn't know or makes multiple errors. You show a card with the correct answer: "123 Maple Street."

***

PROMPT FADING: GRADUALLY REDUCING HELP TO ENCOURAGE THE CHILD'S INDEPENDENCE.

What Is Prompt Fading?

Prompt fading is the process of gradually reducing the level of assistance (or prompts) given to a child so they can perform a skill independently. Since prompts are meant to be temporary, fading helps ensure the child doesn't become dependent on prompt to complete tasks. The goal is to help the child transition from needing assistance to completing the behavior or skill on their own—at the right time and in the right situation. It is up to you to choose which prompt is best for the child according to their needs.

<u>*Why Is Prompt Fading Important?*</u>

- Encourages independence
- Prevents prompt dependency (relying on help to respond)
- Strengthens natural learning and generalization
- Helps the child succeed in real-world settings without adult assistance

Most-to-Least Prompt Fading

This is the most commonly used method for teaching new skills. You start with the most supportive prompt and gradually reduce the level of help until it is no longer necessary.

When to Use:
When the child is learning a new skill
When you want to avoid errors while building early success

How It Works
Begin with a full physical prompt (e.g., hand-over-hand) and move down the prompting hierarchy as the child becomes more independent: Full Physical → Partial Physical → Model → Gesture → Verbal → Textual → Independent

Example: Teaching a Child to Put on a Coat (Most-to-Least Prompt Fading)

- Start by using hand-over-hand assistance to guide the child's arm into the sleeve.
- Next, provide partial physical support by gently guiding their elbow.
- Then, use a modeling prompt by putting on your own coat as the child watches.
- After that, use a gesture prompt by pointing to the coat.
- Finally, give a verbal prompt such as, "Put on your coat," and allow the child to complete the task independently. If the child gets stuck at any point, provide additional verbal guidance, such as, "Put your left arm in the sleeve."

Least-to-Most Prompt Fading

This method gives the child a chance to try independently before receiving help. It works well when the child already has some understanding of the skill but may need occasional support.

When to Use
When re-teaching a skill
When the child might already know what to do
How It Works
Give the instruction and wait. If there's no response, add support, moving from least to most intrusive:
  Instruction → Wait → Verbal → Gesture → Model → Physical → Full Physical
Example: Teaching the Child to Throw Away Trash

- Say: "Put it in the trash," and wait 5 seconds for a response.
- If no response, give a verbal prompt: "Throw it away here."
- If the child still does not act, use a gesture prompt by pointing to the trash can.
- If needed, model the behavior by walking over and throwing away a similar item.
- If the child is still not throwing the garbage, use partial physical prompting by gently touching the wrist or another nearby part of the arm.
- Provide full physical assistance only if necessary to ensure task completion.

Fading Verbal Prompts

This approach gradually reduces how much you say when giving verbal prompts to help the child become less dependent on exact phrases.

How It Works
Start with a full verbal prompt and gradually reduce it:
Full Verbal Prompt → Partial Prompt → Keyword → Wait → Independent response
Example: Verbal Prompt Fading (for a child using phrases):

- Full Verbal Prompt: "Say, 'I want juice,'" and expect the child to say it.
- Partial Verbal Prompt: "Say, 'I want...,'" and expect the child to complete it.
- Keyword Prompt: "I...," and expect the child to finish the phrase independently.
- Then wait silently for the child to respond independently.

Note: This example is for a child who is already using phrases. For a child learning to use one word, the fading process focuses on encouraging complete single words.

- Start with a full word prompt, such as "Say 'juice.'" and expect the child to repeat the word.
- Then use partial or initial sounds as prompts, like "Ju..." and expect the child to complete the word.
- Next, prompt using only the first sound, such as "J..." and expect the child to produce the full word.
- Gradually wait for the child to say the word independently, and expect the child to respond without prompts.

Fading Textual Prompts

Textual prompts use written words, signs, or phrases to support learning and communication, especially for children who know how to read.

<u>When to Use:</u>

Teaching personal information (e.g., name, address, phone number)

Early literacy or academic skills

Textual prompts can be used in many areas because they are easy to fade.

<u>How It Works:</u>

There are different ways to fade textual prompts. Let's learn with an example.

Example: Teaching a Child to Say Their Address
Target: "123 Maple Street"
Step 1: Textual Prompt (Fill-in-the-Blank)

- Start by showing a card with: "123 Maple _____" Expect the child to respond: "123 Maple Street"
- Next, show a card with: "123 Ma_____" Expect the child to respond: "123 Maple Street"
- Then, show a card with: "123 ___" Expect the child to respond: "123 Maple Street"
- Then, show a card with: "1 ___" Expect the child to respond: "123 Maple Street"
- Finally, remove the card and ask, "What's your address?"
- The child responds independently: "123 Maple Street"

Things to Remember

- Always pair fading with reinforcement. Praise or reward correct responses—even when prompted—to keep motivation high.
- Use differential reinforcement: give bigger or preferred rewards for independent responses, smaller ones for prompted responses.
- Watch for prompt dependency. If the child waits for help, consider fading faster or changing strategies.
- Track progress. Use simple notes or data sheets to track prompt levels and independence.
- Individualize. Each child is different—some need slow, careful fading; others progress quickly.

ERROR CORRECTION: WHAT TO DO WHEN THE CHILD MAKES AN ERROR

When the child makes an error, gently guide them to the correct answer without making them feel bad.

How Parents Can Do Error Correction

When the child gives a wrong answer, present the instruction again and prompt immediately by showing the correct response or giving a helpful hint instead of repeating the same thing over and over and letting the child make multiple errors.

Example:

Parent: "What color is this?" (holding a red ball)
Child: "Blue."
Parent: (quiet)
Parent: "What color is this? Red."
Child: "Red."
Parent: "Yes, great job saying red!"

Parent: "What color is this?" (waits 2 seconds)
Child: (no response)
Parent: "Re..."
Child: "Red."
Parent: "Hip hip hooray! It's red!"

Parent: "What color is this?" (waits 3–5 seconds)
Child: "Red"
Parent: "Yes! You said red all by yourself!" and gives the child 1 Skittle—or any preferred item—as a reward. Giving a bigger reward when the child responds independently helps them understand that doing it on their own earns more than responding with help.

Encourage and praise the child when they try again or correct their mistake. Say things like, "Great job trying again, this is red!" or "You got it this time, red color!". Always keep the environment positive and supportive. Avoid scolding or showing frustration—focus on helping your child understand and improve.

CHAPTER 5

Visual Supports

Visual Supports are tools that use images, symbols, or written words to help children understand instructions, follow routines, and communicate more effectively.

FIRST/THEN BOARD

The "First/Then" strategy is a simple and effective way to help children understand what is expected of them and what will happen next. It teaches that when they do something required ("First"), they can then get something they want ("Then"). This approach is especially helpful for children who need extra support with following directions, transitioning between tasks, or learning new routines. The First/Then strategy is also called the Premack Principle or Grandma's Rule.

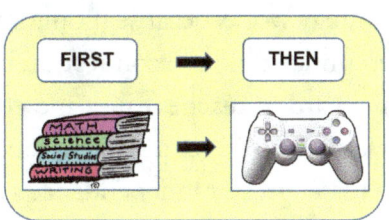

Image 1: First-Then Example

How It Works

This gives structure, sets clear expectations, and motivates the child to complete tasks they might usually avoid. You present the task in this order:

- **First** (something the child needs to do),
- **Then** (something the child enjoys).

Examples

"First clean up your toys, then you get a Skittle." The child knows that once they clean up, they'll earn the reward. It makes the expectation clear and the reward predictable.

Other examples include:

"First finish your homework, then iPad."

"First put on your shoes, then outside time."

"First brush your teeth, then storytime."

Tips for Using First/Then

Keep it simple and specific. Use short, clear phrases.

Use visuals in the beginning, then gradually fade them and rely on verbal instructions only. However, if the child has difficulties, you can continue using visuals for a longer period of time.

Follow through every time. Make sure the child really gets the "Then" once they complete the "First."

Use preferred items as the "Then." Make sure it's something the child actually wants!

The First/Then strategy works because it builds predictability and trust, helping children understand the connection between completing a task and receiving a reward. It teaches cause and effect, supports smoother transitions, and encourages task completion. Over time, using this approach can foster greater independence as children learn to complete activities knowing that something enjoyable will follow.

Token Economy

A Token Economy is a powerful behavioral tool often used in ABA therapy and educational settings to reinforce positive behaviors. It involves giving tokens as immediate rewards for desired behaviors, which can later be exchanged for larger, meaningful rewards. This system helps children develop self-control, motivation, and goal-setting skills while encouraging consistent positive behavior.

Image 2: Token Economy Board

Key Components of a Token Economy

Target Behaviors

These are specific actions or behaviors you want to encourage. Examples include following instructions, completing tasks, using polite language, staying seated during lessons, and cleaning up toys. Clear, measurable behaviors should be chosen so the child knows exactly what is expected.

Tokens

Tokens are tangible symbols or markers given immediately after the child demonstrates the target behavior. Tokens can include stickers, plastic coins, stars on a chart, points on an app, or paper tickets. Tokens should be easy to handle and collect, and visually motivating if possible.

Reinforcers (Backup Rewards)

These are the actual rewards the child earns by exchanging tokens. Reinforcers should be highly motivating to the child, appropriate for their age and preferences, and varied to maintain interest over time. Examples include extra playtime, snacks, small toys, screen time, or special activities.

How to Implement a Token Economy

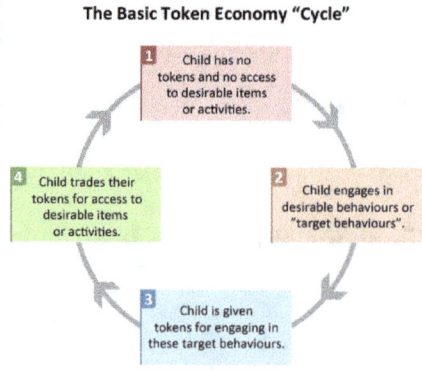

Image 3: The basic token economy cycle

Step 1: Explain the System

Start by clearly explaining the token economy to the child. Let them know which specific behaviors will earn tokens and how many tokens are needed to earn a reward. It's important to check what the child is motivated for—ask directly or conduct a preference assessment to find out what they enjoy. This helps ensure the rewards are meaningful and motivating, increasing the likelihood that the child will engage in the desired behaviors.

Step 2: Immediate Reinforcement

Give tokens immediately after the desired behavior to strengthen the connection between the behavior and the reward.

Step 3: Tracking Tokens

Use a visible token board, chart, or container so the child can see their progress. This visual tracking can increase motivation.

Step 4: Token Exchange

Set a reasonable number of tokens needed for each reward. Allow the child to trade in tokens once they reach the goal.

Step 5: Gradual Fading

As the child's behavior improves, gradually increase the number of tokens required for a reward or shift to more natural reinforcers like verbal praise. This helps maintain behavior without over-reliance on tangible rewards.

Tips for Success

- Personalize Rewards: Tailor reinforcers to each child's interests and needs. What motivates one child may not work for another.
- Consistency: Be consistent in delivering tokens immediately after the target behavior.
- Start Small: Begin with just one or two target behaviors to avoid overwhelming the child.
- Clarity: Keep the system simple and clear to avoid confusion.
- Flexibility: Adjust the program as needed based on the child's progress and preferences.
- Pair with Praise: Always combine tokens with specific verbal praise to enhance learning.

Why Use a Token Economy?

A token economy teaches kids to wait patiently for a reward, which helps build self-control and delayed gratification. It also encourages children to stay motivated and take responsibility for their behavior by showing progress toward a goal. Additionally, the approach is flexible and can be adapted for various settings such as home, school, and therapy sessions. Overall, a token economy keeps children engaged in positive behaviors consistently, making learning and behavior change more effective and enjoyable.

* * *

Visual Schedules

A visual schedule is a tool that shows a sequence of activities, routines, or steps using images, symbols, or written words. It provides a clear, concrete way to help children understand what is happening now, what is coming next, and what is expected of them. Visual schedules are especially helpful for children who benefit from structure, such as those with autism or developmental delays. They support understanding, reduce uncertainty, and promote independence by making daily routines predictable and easier to follow.

<u>Why Are Visual Schedules Important?</u>

Visual schedules support positive behavior and reduce escape or avoidance behaviors by:

- Providing clear expectations: Children know what they're supposed to do and what's coming next, which reduces confusion.
- Improving transitions: Moving from one activity to another can be difficult. Visual cues make transitions smoother.
- Increasing independence: Children learn to follow routines on their own without needing constant verbal reminders.
- Supporting emotional regulation: When children know what to expect, they are less likely to become overwhelmed or avoid tasks.

- Supporting understanding : Visuals are especially helpful for children with limited verbal skills or receptive language delays.

Types of Visual Schedules

Visual schedules can be customized based on your child's needs, age, and level of understanding:

- Whole-day schedules: Show the entire day's activities in order (e.g., Wake up → Brush teeth → Breakfast → School).
- Mini-schedules: Focus on a smaller routine (e.g., Getting dressed: Shirt → Pants → Socks → Shoes).

How to Use a Visual Schedule

- **Create the visuals:** Use photos, symbols, or simple drawings. You can also include written words for children who can read.
- **Introduce the schedule:** Explain it clearly and model how to use it. Say, "Let's check the schedule," and guide your child through each step.
- **Post it in a visible place:** Hang the schedule on a wall or door, or use a portable binder or clipboard.
- **Use it consistently:** Refer to the schedule throughout the day. Point to each step as you go to build the habit.
- **Allow participation:** Let the child move the pieces, check off tasks, or flip cards when a task is done. This reinforces progress.
- **Use real-time feedback:** Provide reinforcement (e.g., praise or a reward) when the child follows the schedule correctly.

Morning Routine Visual Schedule

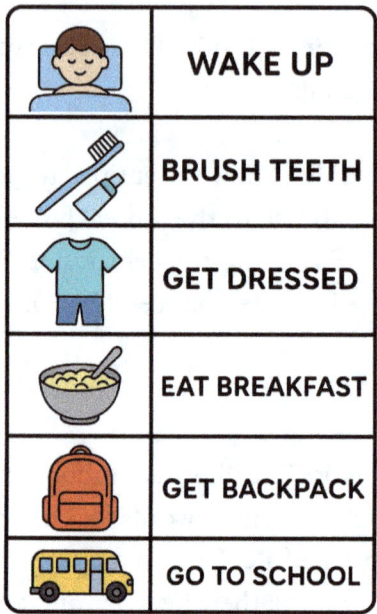

Image 4: Morning visual schedule example

<u>Tips for Success</u>

- Start small: Begin with just 2–3 steps and build up as the child becomes familiar with the routine.
- Use visuals the child understands: Real photos are best for some children; simple icons may work for others.
- Be flexible: Schedules can be adjusted based on the child's day. Use removable pieces like Velcro or magnets.
- Fade prompts gradually: Over time, reduce how often you remind the child to check the schedule.

If the child follows the visual schedule, don't forget to reinforce or reward their behavior—this helps maintain motivation and increases the likelihood they'll continue using the schedule successfully.

***

VISUAL TIMERS

Visual timers display the passage of time in a way that children can easily understand. They help children see how much time is left for an activity or when a transition will happen. Timers can be physical tools, such as digital clocks or timers on your phone, as well as digital timers found in many apps.

Image 5: Visual Timers

Why Use Visual Timers?

Many children find it difficult to transition from preferred activities (like iPad time) to non-preferred ones (like work time). The brain needs time to process the change, and sudden transitions can feel overwhelming. Visual timers make time more clear and predictable, helping reduce anxiety and making it easier for children to understand when one activity will end and another will begin.

<u>How Visual Timers Help</u>

- Show how much time remains for an activity
- Help children prepare for upcoming transitions
- Teach patience and waiting skills
- Encourage independence by letting children monitor time themselves

CHAPTER 6

Structured Choice-Making

STRUCTURED CHOICE-MAKING

Structured choice-making is an evidence-based ABA strategy that helps children gain a sense of control and autonomy by offering them limited, guided options to choose from. This method balances giving the child freedom to decide while maintaining clear boundaries and expectations.

<u>Why It Works</u>

Children often resist demands when they feel they have no control. Structured choices reduce power struggles by offering some autonomy within clear boundaries. This approach builds cooperation, improves decision-making, and supports self-regulation.

<u>How Structured Choice-Making Supports Learning and Behavior</u>

- **Increases cooperation:** When children feel heard and involved, they are more likely to cooperate willingly rather than resist or refuse.
- **Builds decision-making skills:** Making choices helps children practice thinking through options and consequences.
- **Enhances independence:** Choosing between acceptable options encourages self-regulation and confidence.

- **Reduces challenging behavior:** Power struggles and refusal often decrease when children have some control over what happens to them.
- **Promotes engagement:** Children are more engaged when they feel their preferences matter.

Steps to Implement Structured Choice-Making

- **Identify the task or behavior you want to encourage:** Decide what you want the child to do. For example, you want the child to finish both their English and Math homework.
- **Select 2 to 3 acceptable options:** Offer choices that lead to the same goal. For example:
  "Do you want to start with English or Math homework?"
  "Do you want to do your homework sitting at the table or lying on the mat?"
- **Present the options clearly and simply:** Use short phrases or visuals:
  Show the Math book and English notebook and ask, "Which one first?"
  If the child understands verbal instructions, you can simply say, "Do you want to start with English or Math homework?"
- **Encourage the child to choose:** Give them time to choose and avoid rushing. If needed, provide a gentle prompt.
- **Follow through consistently:** Once they choose, support their choice: "Great! Let's start English first like you picked."
- **If the child doesn't choose, select for them:** If the child delays or avoids choosing, you can say: "I'll choose this time. Let's start with Math, and next time you can pick."

Examples of Structured Choice-Making

- **Morning Routine:** "Would you like to brush your teeth first or get dressed first?"
- **Snack Time:** "Do you want apple slices or banana for your snack?"
- **Homework:** "Do you want to do your reading or math homework first?"
- **Playtime:** "Would you like to play with blocks or coloring first?"
- **Cleaning Up:** "Would you like to put away the books or the toys first?"

Tips for Success

- Use visuals like pictures or choice boards if the child is nonverbal or learns better visually.
- Keep choices limited to avoid overwhelming the child—two or three options are ideal.
- Make sure all choices are acceptable to you so the child isn't given an option that leads to refusal or disruption.
- Use an enthusiastic and positive tone to make choices inviting and motivating.

Choice Boards

What Is a Choice Board?

A choice board is a visual tool that offers children a selection of options to choose from. It helps them communicate their preferences, make decisions, and feel more in control of their environment.

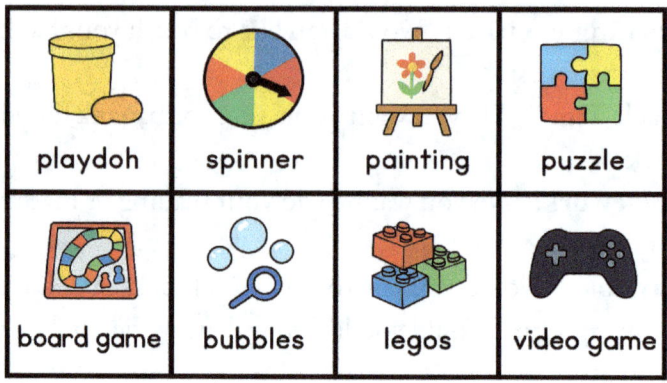

Image 1: Choice Board

Why Use Choice Boards?

Choice boards promote independence and reduce stress by giving children clear options. They are especially useful for children who have difficulty expressing themselves verbally or who benefit from visual supports.

How Choice Boards Help

- Encourage communication and decision-making skills.
- Increase motivation by allowing the child to pick preferred activities or items
- Reduce problem behaviors by offering acceptable choices.
- Support self-regulation by giving a sense of control

How to Use a Choice Board

- Create a board with pictures, symbols, or words representing options

- Present the board clearly and allow the child to select by pointing, touching, or vocally saying it
- Reinforce the child's choice by providing the selected item or activity
- Update and rotate options regularly to maintain interest

CHAPTER 7

Teaching Complex Skills using shaping and chaining

WHAT IS SHAPING?

Shaping is a behavioral technique used to teach new skills by reinforcing closer and closer approximations of the desired behavior. Instead of expecting a child to perform a skill perfectly right away, shaping breaks the task into smaller, more manageable steps. Each small step that gets closer to the desired behavior is reinforced until the child can perform the full skill independently.

This technique is especially helpful for teaching complex or difficult behaviors because it allows children to build on what they already know. Shaping is gradual and encourages the child's development by reinforcing even the smallest progress.

How Shaping Works
- **Build Confidence:** Children gain confidence as they make graadual progress toward mastering new skills. Reinforcing small successes helps them feel good and motivates them to keep trying.
- **Gradually raise the bar:** Once the child has mastered a step, move to the next one. For example, after holding the cup, rein-

force the child for bringing it to their mouth, then sipping from it, and finally drinking from it without spilling.
- **Reinforce progress:** Reinforce the step that the child is learning, not the mastered one. By consistently rewarding each closer approximation, the child will gradually learn to perform the full behavior correctly over time.
- **Be patient and consistent:** Shaping takes time, so celebrate small successes along the way. Consistent reinforcement will keep the child motivated to keep working toward the goal.

Why Shaping is Important in Teaching Skills

- **Builds confidence:** Children gain confidence as they make gradual progress toward mastering new skills. Reinforcing small successes helps them feel good about their progress and motivates them to keep trying.
- **Encourages learning:** Shaping allows children to learn in small steps, which is easier and less overwhelming. It helps prevent frustration if they can't do the whole skill right away.
- **Teaches complex behaviors:** Shaping is ideal for teaching complex behaviors like language skills, social interactions, and motor skills, which often require breaking them down into smaller parts.
- **Promotes self-confidence:** As children master each step, they gain a sense of achievement, which builds their confidence and encourages further learning.
- <u>*Example 1:*</u> Teaching a Child to Say "Apple"

Step 1: Reinforce the child for making any sound close to the word *"apple."* For example, if the child says "ah," say, "Nice job saying 'ah!'" and give a reward, such as a Skittle or a brief play session with a favorite toy.

Step 2: After a few days, once the child has mastered saying "ah," stop reinforcing just that sound. Reinforce when the child says "ap." Say, "Great job saying 'ap!'" and give a similar reward.

Step 3: After a few more days, once the child has mastered saying "ap," stop reinforcing only that sound. Reinforce when the child says "apple" correctly. Say, "Awesome! You said 'apple!'" and offer a larger reward, like extra playtime or more Skittles.

Image 1: Shaping example to help a child in speaking the word "Apple"

Example 2: Teaching a Child to Drink from a Cup

Step 1: Reinforce holding the cup, even if the child is not drinking yet. Say, "Nice job holding the cup!" and reward with a favorite treat or toy.

Step 2: After a few days, once the child has mastered holding the cup, stop reinforcing just that. Reinforce bringing the cup to the mouth. Say, "Good job bringing the cup to your mouth!" and give a reward.

Step 3: After a few more days, once the child has mastered bringing the cup to the mouth, stop reinforcing only that step. Reinforce taking a sip from the cup. Say, "Great job taking a sip!" and give a reward.

Step 4: After a few more days, once the child has mastered sipping, stop reinforcing only that step. Reinforce drinking independently without spilling. Say, "Awesome! You drank the whole cup!" and give a bigger reward.

<u>Example 3:</u> Shaping Social Behaviors (e.g., Greeting Someone)

Step 1: Reinforce looking at a person when greeted, even if the child does not say anything yet. Say, "Nice job looking at the person!" and give a favorite treat or toy.

Step 2: After a few days, once the child has mastered looking, stop reinforcing just that. Reinforce saying something like "hi" or waving, even if unclear. Say, "Good job saying 'hi'!" and give a reward.

Step 3: After a few more days, once the child has mastered saying "hi" or waving, stop reinforcing only that step. Reinforce saying "hi" while making eye contact. Say, "Great job saying 'hi' and looking at them!" and give a reward.

Step 4: After a few more days, once the child has mastered eye contact, stop reinforcing only that step. Reinforce giving a full greeting like, "Hi, how are you?" and waiting for a response. Say, "Awesome! You said 'hi' and asked how they are!" and give a bigger reward.

Why Shaping Matters in Teaching

Shaping is a powerful technique for teaching a wide range of important skills. It helps children learn complex behaviors step by step, reinforcing progress along the way. By using shaping, you can build a child's skills, boost their confidence, and provide the support they need to succeed. With patience, consistency, and positive reinforcement, shaping encourages children to master new skills at their own pace while celebrating every small accomplishment.

CHAINING

What Is Chaining?

Chaining is a teaching strategy used in Applied Behavior Analysis (ABA) to help children learn complex tasks by breaking them down into smaller, manageable steps. Think about daily routines like:

- Brushing teeth
- Getting dressed
- Washing hands
- Tying shoes
- Packing a backpack

These routines involve many steps. Learning them all at once can feel overwhelming—especially for children with developmental delays or autism. Chaining teaches one step at a time, helping the child build independence and confidence. There are multiple types of chaining which we will discuss later in the chapter.

Why Use Chaining?
Chaining is helpful because it:

- Breaks big tasks into small, teachable pieces
- Builds confidence through small successes
- Reduces frustration by not expecting perfection
- Encourages independence in daily life

Task Example: Washing Hands
Let's break hand washing into 7 steps:

1. Turn on the faucet
2. Wet hands
3. Get soap
4. Rub hands together

5. Rinse hands
6. Turn off the faucet
7. Dry hands

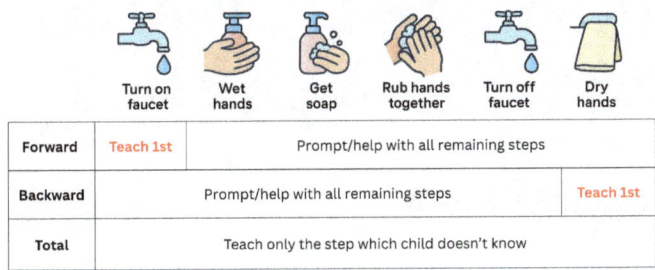

Image 2: Chaining method to teach a child on hand washing

Types of Chaining

Forward Chaining

You teach the first step in the task and help with the rest. As the child learns, you teach the next step—always starting from the beginning.

<u>How It Works:</u>

- Teach Step 1 (e.g., turning on the faucet) by guiding the child if needed, and help with Steps 2–7 using full physical prompts (hand-over-hand or any support the child is comfortable with) without expecting independent performance of these steps.
- Once Step 1 is mastered and the child can do it independently, teach Step 2 (wetting hands), and continue.
- Add one new step at a time until the full task is learned.

Example:

- Teach Step 1 (turning on the faucet), and help with Steps 2–7 using full physical prompts (hand-over-hand or any support the child is comfortable with).
- Once Step 1 (turning on the faucet) is mastered and the child can do it independently, teach Step 2 (wetting hands), and continue help with Steps 3–7 using full physical prompts.
- Now that the child can independently complete Step 1 (turning on the faucet) and Step 2 (wetting hands), teach Step 3 (applying soap), and continue. Help with Steps 4–7 using full physical prompts.
- Repeat this process, adding one new step at a time, until the child can wash their hands independently from beginning to end.

Forward Chaining is best for:

- Children who already know or can do the first few steps.
- Learners who benefit from structured, step-by-step teaching.
- Children who need strong support early in the task.

Backward Chaining

You teach the last step first and help with all the remaining steps. Once the last step is mastered, you teach the second-last step, and so on—adding one earlier step at a time.

How It Works:

- Help the child with Steps 1–6 using full physical prompts (hand-over-hand or any support the child is comfortable with).
- Teach Step 7 (e.g., drying hands) by guiding the child if needed.

- Once the child can do Step 7 independently, teach Step 6 (e.g., rinsing hands), and continue.
- Add one earlier step at a time, working backward, until the child can complete the entire task independently.

Example:

- You help the child from Step 1 (turning on the faucet) through Step 6 (turning off the faucet). The child completes Step 7 (drying hands) independently.
- If the child has mastered the last step, they now complete the last two steps independently — Step 6 (turning off the faucet) and Step 7 (drying hands).

Continue: Gradually teach earlier steps until the child can complete the full handwashing routine independently.

Backward Chaining is best for:

- Children who struggle to begin learning a new skill
- Learners who don't yet understand the full task
- Those who are motivated by finishing tasks
- The most popular chaining method in ABA

Total Task Chaining

You teach the entire routine at once. The child tries every step, and you help only when needed. Over time, your help is reduced as they improve.

How It Works:

- Present the full task (e.g., handwashing)
- Child attempts all 7 steps
- Give help only for steps they don't know

- Fade support gradually as they gain confidence

Example:

- Child does all 7 steps with help as needed
- Next time, child does more steps on their own
- Continue until the child is independent with the full task

Total task analysis is best for:

- Children who already know some steps
- Learners with the attention span to complete full routines

CHAPTER 8

Toilet Training

TOILET TRAINING

Toilet training is an important life skill for children. It can be taught effectively using consistent routines, clear instructions, and positive reinforcement. Some children may learn quickly, while others may need extra time and practice — and that's okay! Below is a detailed, step-by-step plan that combines professional strategies and real-life tips for success.

<u>*Make Sure the child is ready*</u>
If the child -

- Around 2 years old (readiness may vary by child).
- Can stay dry for at least 30 minutes to 45 minutes at a time.
- Able to walk and sit independently on a toilet or potty.
- Understands and follows simple instructions.
- Is free from medical issues like UTIs.
- Can communicate needs (verbally or through gestures).

Materials You'll Need

- Potty chair or toilet seat insert.
- Training pants (cloth underwear) or regular underwear.
- Lots of fluids (juice, water, etc.).
- Preferred snacks and small rewards (stickers, tokens, praise).
- Wet wipes and spare clothes.
- Optional: A doll or any of their favorite toys (for modeling).

Demo: Using a Doll or Their Favorite Toy (e.g., Froggy) for Demonstration (Optional)

Before beginning the training day, it's helpful to use a doll or a favorite toy to demonstrate the toileting process. This gives the child a clear visual example of what to do. Show the doll sitting on the potty, wiping, flushing, and washing hands. These demonstrations help the child understand each step before trying it themselves, making the transition to real toileting smoother and less intimidating.

Step 1: Preparation

The first step in toilet training is to prepare the child for the training day. Before starting, ensure that the child is healthy and free from medical issues such as urinary tract infections (UTIs), as these can affect the training process. When planning to begin toilet training, stop using regular diapers and switch to underpants or training diapers. Regular diapers prevent the child from feeling wet, which can hinder the learning process.

Step 2: Fluid Intake

To start, give the child plenty of fluids. This step ensures that they will need to use the toilet frequently throughout the day. Offering drinks every 30 minutes to an hour keeps the child hydrated and ensures they will be prompted to use the potty regularly. The goal is to create multiple opportunities for the child to practice using the toilet.

Potty Training Guidelines

Take the child to the potty at regular intervals. At the beginning, it's recommended to take them every 15 minutes and have them sit for about 5-10 minutes each time. When you bring the child to the toilet, use a consistent verbal cue like, "It's time to go potty," or use a sign to let them know it's time for a bathroom visit. This routine helps the child understand what to expect and builds a consistent habit, which increases the chances of success.

Start with 15-minute intervals and observe how long your child stays dry. Once you notice the child usually urinates at predictable times—such as every 30 minutes—you can gradually extend the interval to 25 or 30 minutes to reduce accidents while still reinforcing the routine.

Even if the child doesn't show signs of needing to go, sticking to a consistent schedule gives them many chances to practice and reinforces that the bathroom is the right place to go.

During each potty visit, encourage the child to try to pee in the toilet. If they do, provide an immediate reward such as iPad time, playing with a favorite toy, a Skittle, etc. If they don't go, avoid scolding. Instead, say, 'Great try! Remember, if you need to pee, use the toilet,' and no reward is given.

Tip for Missed Attempts

If the child does not urinate at the scheduled time, try again after 10 minutes to help prevent accidents. Then, adjust your schedule accordingly. For example, if you took the child at 6:00 PM but they didn't pee, try again at 6:10 PM. If they successfully urinate at that time, and you're following a 30-minute interval, your next potty time would be around 6:40 PM.

You might wonder: "How will the child learn to go on their own?"

Independent initiation usually develops later. Early in toilet training, the focus is on building a routine and helping the child become aware of their body signals. By taking the child regularly to the potty, you help them connect the feeling of needing to go with using the toilet.

As the child becomes more familiar with the process and gains better bladder control, they will show signs that they need to go, such as stopping an activity, holding themselves, or telling you verbally. Like any skill, learning to initiate takes time, patience, consistency, and plenty of positive reinforcement. With practice, the child will learn to recognize their own needs and use the bathroom independently.

Step 3: Positive Reinforcement

When the child successfully uses the toilet, immediately provide positive reinforcement. This can be in the form of praise, a small reward, or a favorite activity. The key is to celebrate every success to build motivation.

Step 4: Positive Practice for Accidents

In the famous book *Toileting in Less Than a Day*, it is mentioned that positive practice for accidents is an important step in toilet training. Positive practice means that when an accident occurs, we quickly take the child from the spot of the accident to the toilet and back again 3–4 times. However, it is important to note that this is not something to use in the initial stages of toilet training. Additionally, most children may not require positive practice at all, as their training may progress without this step.

Step 5: Data Recording

Keeping a record of all successful trips and accidents is important to understand the child's progress, identify patterns, and make necessary adjustments to the training plan. We also track dry checks, which involve observing and noting whether the child remains dry between scheduled potty visits. Don't forget to praise them during this time, saying things like, "I'm proud of you that your underpants are dry!"

Toilet Training Tracking Sheet

Time	Pull-up			Underwear			Toilet			Self-Initiated (Yes/No)	Comments
	pee	BM	dry	pee	BM	dry	pee	BM	no void		
	pee	BM	dry	pee	BM	dry	pee	BM	no void		
	pee	BM	dry	pee	BM	dry	pee	BM	no void		
	pee	BM	dry	pee	BM	dry	pee	BM	no void		
	pee	BM	dry	pee	BM	dry	pee	BM	no void		
	pee	BM	dry	pee	BM	dry	pee	BM	no void		
	pee	BM	dry	pee	BM	dry	pee	BM	no void		
	pee	BM	dry	pee	BM	dry	pee	BM	no void		
	pee	BM	dry	pee	BM	dry	pee	BM	no void		
	pee	BM	dry	pee	BM	dry	pee	BM	no void		
	pee	BM	dry	pee	BM	dry	pee	BM	no void		
	pee	BM	dry	pee	BM	dry	pee	BM	no void		
	pee	BM	dry	pee	BM	dry	pee	BM	no void		
	pee	BM	dry	pee	BM	dry	pee	BM	no void		
	pee	BM	dry	pee	BM	dry	pee	BM	no void		
	pee	BM	dry	pee	BM	dry	pee	BM	no void		
	pee	BM	dry	pee	BM	dry	pee	BM	no void		
	pee	BM	dry	pee	BM	dry	pee	BM	no void		
	pee	BM	dry	pee	BM	dry	pee	BM	no void		
	pee	BM	dry	pee	BM	dry	pee	BM	no void		
	pee	BM	dry	pee	BM	dry	pee	BM	no void		
	pee	BM	dry	pee	BM	dry	pee	BM	no void		
	pee	BM	dry	pee	BM	dry	pee	BM	no void		

Toilet Training Tracking Sheet
Credit: Surrey Place

Here are several effective strategies to support toileting skills in young children

Read Toilet Training Books

Introduce potty concepts with fun and engaging children's books. Stories with relatable characters and simple explanations can help children understand the process, reduce anxiety, and build motivation.

Books like *"Potty"* by Leslie Patricelli or *"Once Upon a Potty"* by Alona Frankel are great starting points.

<u>Involve Favorite Toys</u>

Encourage the child to "teach" their favorite stuffed animal or toy how to use the potty. This playful method boosts confidence and helps the child feel in control.

<u>Watch Child-Friendly Potty Videos</u>

Short animated videos can visually model potty behaviors in a way that's fun and easy to understand, especially for visual learners.

<u>Sticker Charts and Rewards</u>

Use a reward system with stickers for each successful attempt. After earning a set number, the child can receive a small prize or special treat, building motivation.

<u>Choose Fun Underwear</u>

Let the child pick out "big kid" underwear with favorite characters. This makes them excited about the transition and gives them a sense of responsibility.

<u>Use Toileting Language Consistently</u>

Use the same words like "pee," "poop," "potty," or "toilet" consistently. This helps the child learn and communicate their needs clearly.

* * *

TEACHING BOWEL MOVEMENTS ON THE TOILET

Helping the child learn to poop on the toilet often takes more time and patience than teaching urination. Many children feel unsure or even fearful about using the toilet for bowel movements. With a calm, consistent approach, the child can develop this important life skill.

Step 1: Observe and Track Patterns

Before beginning active teaching, spend a few days tracking the child's natural bowel movement habits Knowing their usual pattern helps you predict the best time to encourage toilet use:

- Time of day they usually go
- Body language cues like squatting, hiding, or becoming very still
- Pre-pooping behaviors like grunting, holding their bottom, or pausing during play

Step 2: Introduce Scheduled Bathroom Sits

- Once you've identified the child's likely bowel movement times—such as usually going after meals—take them to the toilet 10–30 minutes after eating.
- Let them sit on the toilet for 5–10 minutes, even if nothing happens.
- Keep the environment relaxed and pressure-free by reading a short book, singing a song, or letting them hold a comfort toy.
- Use a footrest to help them feel secure and to support proper posture.

Step 3: Celebrate All Efforts and Successes

- Reinforce all positive steps like sitting on the toilet, telling you they need to poop, or successfully using the toilet.
- Give specific praise such as "You did a great job sitting on the potty!" or "I'm proud of you for trying!"
- Offer motivating rewards like stickers, favorite snacks or toys, or extra storytime/screen time.
- Use a visual chart to track progress and celebrate successes.

Step 4: Handle Accidents Calmly

Accidents are normal during the learning process. When one happens:

- Stay calm and avoid punishment or frustration
- Say something simple like, "Poop goes in the toilet."
- Help clean up if the child is ready, and gently encourage them to try again next time

Step 5: Build the Full Bathroom Routine

Following the same routine each time builds confidence and independence. As the child becomes more comfortable:

- Teach wiping
- Practice flushing
- Reinforce hand washing with soap and water

Step 6: Encourage Independent Initiation

At first, you'll guide most of the process. Over time:

- Watch for signs and encourage the child to tell you
- Use prompts like: "Do you feel like you need to poop?"
- Reinforce every attempt at independence
- Slowly reduce your prompts as they become more consistent

Final Tips for Success:

- Offer plenty of water and fiber to support regular bowel movements
- Avoid stool holding—constipation can make toilet training harder
- Celebrate small steps as big wins

***

NIGHTTIME TOILET TRAINING

Nighttime potty training usually takes longer than daytime training. This is because the child's bladder needs to hold urine overnight, and the child must wake up when they need to go.

Signs that a child may be ready include waking up dry for several nights in a row. Patience, positivity, and encouragement are essential—punishing a child for accidents can make progress more difficult. Nighttime accidents are common up to around age seven or eight. If a child over age 9 continues to wet the bed or regresses after being trained, it is advisable to consult a healthcare professional.

Key Strategies for Nighttime Potty Training

Monitor Dry Nights
Keep track of nights when the child wakes up dry. Consistent dry nights are a good indicator that the child may be ready to try underwear at night.

Limit Fluid Intake Before Bed
Encourage the child to drink plenty of fluids during the day, but reduce drinks in the evening to help prevent nighttime accidents.

Establish a Bedtime Routine
Have the child use the toilet right before bed. This routine signals to the body that it is time to empty the bladder.

Use Nighttime Protection
Until the child consistently stays dry, consider using nighttime underwear or training pants to manage accidents and provide comfort.

Make the Bathroom Accessible
Ensure the child can reach the toilet easily. Leave doors open, use a nightlight, and place a step stool if needed.

Be Patient and Supportive
Accidents are a normal part of the learning process. Offer praise for effort and progress, and avoid scolding.

Consult a Pediatrician if Needed
If bedwetting continues beyond age nine, consult a healthcare professional to rule out any medical concerns.

Use a Potty Alarm (Optional)
A potty alarm is a small moisture-sensing device that attaches to the child's underwear or pull-up:

- It beeps when wetness is detected, helping the child wake and use the toilet.
- Over time, this builds awareness of body signals and encourages independent waking somewhere.

Transitioning to Underwear at Night

Once the child consistently wakes up dry, it is time to transition from diapers or pull-ups to underwear at night.

Remove Nighttime Diapers Gradually: Begin by skipping diapers during naps, and then move to nighttime when the child shows readiness.

Use Waterproof Mattress Protectors: Protect the bed in case of accidents while the child adjusts.

Maintain a Consistent Routine: Continue the bedtime routine of using the toilet and limiting evening fluids.

Offer Positive Reinforcement: Praise the child for staying dry and encourage continued progress.

CHAPTER 9

Behavioral Contracts

WHAT IS A BEHAVIORAL CONTRACT?

A behavioral contract is a written agreement between a child and an adult (such as a parent, teacher, or therapist). It clearly outlines what behavior is expected, when it should happen, how it will be measured, and what reward (or consequence) will follow. This tool helps children stay motivated, build responsibility, and understand the link between their actions and outcomes.

A well-designed behavioral contract includes four essential components:

1. Identifying the Target Behavior

This is the specific behavior the child is expected to do. It should be clear, observable, and something the child can control. Example: "I will complete my school homework by the assigned time."

2. When the Behavior Must Be Performed

This part explains the time or situation in which the behavior should happen. Example: "Every weekday evening, before 7:00 PM."

3. How the Behavior Will Be Measured

This explains how adults will know if the behavior occurred and who will check it. Example: "My parent will check each evening at 7:00 PM to see if I have completed all of my school homework for the day."

4. Reinforcement Contingency

This outlines what reward the child will earn for completing the behavior—or what happens if they don't. Example: "If I complete all of my school homework on time, I will earn 30 minutes of screen time or a reward of my choice. If I don't complete my homework, I will not get the reward that day."

Why Is It Mostly Used for Older Kids?

Behavioral contracts are especially helpful for older children (around age 8 and up). At this age, children can better:

- Understand written agreements
- Connect actions to consequences or rewards
- Take responsibility for their behavior
- Stay motivated to earn meaningful rewards

Behavioral contracts support independence, teach goal-setting, and help older kids follow through with tasks like homework, chores, or self-care routines. Here is one example for homework completion activity (Sample 1)

Behavioral Contract

Activity: Homework Completion

Involved Parties

Child: [Child's Name]
Adult: [Parent/Teacher's Name]

Target Behavior

I will complete all of my school homework assigned by my teacher on time.

When the Behavior Must Be Performed

Every weekday after school, and completed by 7:00 PM.

How the Behavior Will Be Measured

My parent will check each evening at 7:00 PM to see if I have completed all of my school homework for the day.

Reinforcement Contingency

"If I've finished all my school homework on time, I'll get 30 minutes of screen time or a reward I choose. If I don't finish my homework, I won't get the reward that day."

Child's Signature: _____
Adult's Signature: _____
Date _____

Addressing Challenging Behaviors

Until now, we have focused on building the child's learning skills and teaching helpful skills. However, children often engage in challenging or unsafe behaviors that interfere with learning and daily life. These behaviors occur for different reasons, and understanding why a behavior happens is the first step in helping the child. This process is called finding the function of behavior—essentially, what the child is trying to communicate or achieve through their actions.

In the next section, we will explore the common reasons behind these behaviors and learn how to respond in a calm, supportive way. You'll also discover simple strategies to reduce problem behaviors and teach the child better ways to meet their needs.

CHAPTER 10

Behavior: What & Why

WHAT IS BEHAVIOR?

Behavior is anything a person does or says that can be seen, heard, or measured. In ABA, we only call something a "behavior" if it's observable (you can see or hear it happen) and measurable (you can count it or time how long it lasts).

Examples:

- A child clapping hands
- Saying "I want juice"
- Hitting the table
- Walking away
- Putting toys in a box

Non-examples of behavior (not observable directly):

- Feeling angry
- Being lazy
- Having a bad attitude.

These may *influence* behavior, but they are not behaviors themselves in ABA terms because we can't observe or measure them directly.

Why Does Behavior Happen? (Understanding the Function)

All behavior happens for a reason. When we understand the reason (called the function), we can respond in a way that helps the child learn a better or safer behavior. There are four main functions of behavior:

Image 1: Functions of behavior

Attention
The child behaves in a way to gain social interaction or attention from others.

Example: A child screams when a parent is on the phone or talking with someone to get attention.

Access to Tangibles
The child behaves in order to get something they want, such as a toy, snack, tablet, or any preferred item.

Example: A child cries to get something like chips, chocolate, an iPad—or anything else he/she want at that moment.

Escape or Avoidance
The child behaves to avoid or get out of something (like a task, demand, or sensory experience).

Example: A child throws the pencil to avoid doing homework.

Sensory or Automatic
The behavior feels good to the child or meets a sensory need. It is not dependent on anyone else.

Example: A child flaps their hands because it feels calming.

SEAT is a commonly used acronym to help remember the four functions of behavior:

- **S – Sensory**
- **E – Escape**
- **A – Attention**
- **T – Tangibles**

<u>Why Is Identifying the Function Important?</u>
Knowing why a behavior is happening helps us:

- Choose the right strategy to reduce the problem behavior
- Teach a better behavior that serves the same function
- Avoid making the problem worse by reinforcing the wrong thing

- Support the child in a way that is safe, compassionate, and effective

<u>Example</u>:
Child starts throwing a tantrum. It could be because of any reason, like:

- Escape: They don't want to clean.
- Attention: They want you to react.
- Tangible: They want to get a toy or snack from you.
- Sensory: Throwing feels good or makes a fun noise.

Once we understand which of these is the true reason, we can build a plan that works.

* * *

What Is the ABC of Behavior?

To understand and identify the exact function of behaviors, we need to observe the pattern of what happens before, during, and after the behavior and record this data. This helps us effectively manage challenging behaviors. This method is called the ABC approach:

- A – Antecedent: What happens right before the behavior.
- B – Behavior: What the child does (the behavior itself).
- C – Consequence: What happens immediately after the behavior.

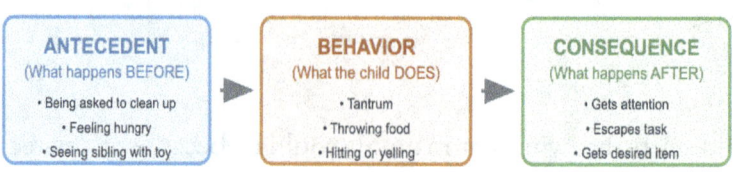

Image 2: ABC model of behavior

A – Antecedent (What Happens Before the Behavior)
The antecedent is the trigger—anything that happens right before the behavior. It could be:

- A demand or instruction ("Time to clean up")
- The removal of a toy or device
- A transition (leaving the park, stopping a game)
- Someone saying "no" to the child

Ask yorself: What happened just before the behavior started?

B – Behavior (The *Action* You Observe)
The behavior is what the child does or says. It must be something you can see or hear, and it should be described clearly and specifically.

Examples:

- Cried and lay on the floor.
- Hit the table with a toy.
- Kicked an adult/peer.

Ask yourself: What exactly did the child do or say? Avoid vague words like "mad" or "being aggressive."

C – Consequence (What Happens After the Behavior)

The consequence is whatever happens immediately after the behavior. This could include:

- Getting attention (even if it's negative)
- Getting access to a toy, snack, or break
- Avoiding or escaping a task
- Being ignored or redirected

Ask yourself: What changed after the behavior happened? Did the child get something or avoid something?

Why This Is Helpful

When we observe the ABCs of behavior, we start to understand the function or purpose of the behavior—why the child is doing it.

Understanding the pattern helps us:

- Prevent the behavior in the future
- Change what happens before or after
- Teach the child a better way to get their needs met

A – Before	B – Behavior	C – After
Asked to stop playing	Child screams and cries	Parent allows more playtime
Told to sit for homework	Child runs away	Task is delayed
Peer takes a toy	Child hits peer	Peer walks away, child gets toy

Below are common examples of antecedents, behaviors, and consequences frequently observed in children. If your observations do not correspond with these examples, please record exactly what occurs in the data sheet.

Antecedent *(What happened before the behavior?)* Check all that apply	**Behavior** *(What did the child do?)* Check all that apply	**Consequence** *(What happened after the behavior?)* Check all that apply
• Asked to stop a preferred activity • Denied access to item/activity • Given a demand/instruction • Transition between activities • Left alone / no attention • Loud/noisy environment • Told "no" • Waiting • Other: _____	• Yelled/screamed • Cried • Hit/kicked/bit • Threw items • Dropped to the floor • Ran away • Said "no" or refused • Ignored instruction • Other: _____	• Given attention • Removed from task/demand stopped • Given item or activity • Redirected to another activity • Ignored • Given a break • Told "no" • Other: _____

Date & Time	Antecedent (What happened before the behavior?)	Behavior (What did the child do?)	Consequence (What happened after the behavior?)

Table 1: ABC Data Sheet Sample

How We Measure Behavior

To find out if a behavior is improving (going down) or getting worse (going up) after starting an intervention, it's important to measure it correctly. BCBAs use many ways to track behaviors. To make this easier for parents, here are some simple and helpful methods to measure behavior at home.

1. Frequency – How many times did it happen?
What it means: Count how many times the child does the behavior.
Example: The child threw toys 3 times during play.
When to use: For quick, countable actions like hitting, yelling, or grabbing.
How to track: Keep a tally mark on paper or use a clicker each time the behavior happens.

2. Rate – How many times per minute or hour?

What it means: How often the behavior happens within a certain time.

Example: The child cried 4 times in 2 hours (that's 2 times per hour).

When to use: When you want to compare behavior during different time periods.

How to track: Count the number of times and note the total time observed. Divide frequency by time (e.g., 4 cries ÷ 2 hours = 2 per hour).

3. Duration – How long did the behavior last?

What it means: The total amount of time the child engages in the behavior.

Example: The child cried for 5 minutes during nap time.

When to use: For behaviors that last some time, like tantrums, crying, or focused play.

How to track: Use a stopwatch or clock to measure how long the behavior lasts from start to finish.

4. Latency – How long did it take for the behavior to start?

What it means: The time between a request or cue and when the child begins the behavior.

Example: You asked the child to put away toys, and they started after 30 seconds.

When to use: To measure how quickly the child responds to instructions.

How to track: Start a timer as soon as you give the instruction, stop when the child starts the behavior.

5. Inter-Response Time (IRT) – How much time passed between behaviors?

What it means: The time between one behavior ending and the next behavior starting.

Example: The child threw a tantrum, then after 10 minutes, threw another.

When to use: To see if behaviors happen closer together or farther apart, especially repeated ones.

How to track: Note the time when one behavior ends and when the next begins. Calculate the time between these.

Measure	What it means	When to use it	How to track
Frequency	How many times behavior happens	Quick, countable actions like hitting, yelling	Tally marks or clicker for each behavior occurrence
Rate	Times per minute or hour	Compare behavior over different time periods	Count occurrences ÷ total observation time
Duration	How long behavior lasts	Longer behaviors like tantrums, crying	Use stopwatch to measure start to end time
Latency	Time to start behavior after cue	How fast your child responds to instructions	Timer from instruction to behavior start
IRT	Time between behaviors	Time gap between repeated behaviors	Record end and start times of behaviors, calculate gap

Table 2: Behavior Measurement Methods: Definitions, Uses, and Tracking

Once you've collected ABC data (Antecedent–Behavior–Consequence) and measured how often the behavior occurs, the next step is to analyze the data to understand why the child is engaging in that behavior. This is referred to as the function of the behavior. Identifying the function helps you respond in ways that support the child in learning more appropriate skills, while gradually reducing challenging behaviors. Ongoing measurement also allows you to track progress and determine whether your intervention is effective.

Now it's time to review your ABC data sheet and identify patterns. Ask yourself: Is the child engaging in the behavior to gain attention, escape a task, access a preferred item (such as a toy or snack), or meet a sensory need?

If your answers mostly match below section, the function may be Attention

Antecedent (Before Behavior)	Behavior (What Child Did)	Consequence (What Happened After)
• Parent talking to someone else • Sibling got attention • Parent busy with work	• Yelled • Interrupted • Hit • Any behavior	• Parent gave attention, either positive or negative. • Child was scolded

If your answers mostly match below section, the function may be Escape or Avoidance

Antecedent (Before Behavior)	Behavior (What Child Did)	Consequence (What Happened After)
• Task given • Told to clean up • Transition warning	• Dropped to floor • Ran away • Tantrum • Any behavior	• Task removed • Given a break • Task represented

If your answers mostly match below section, the function may be Tangible

Antecedent (Before Behavior)	Behavior (What Child Did)	Consequence (What Happened After)
• Told 'no' • Item taken away • Couldn't access desired toy/food • Had to wait	• Screamed • Cried • Hit • Any behavior	• Received item • Distracted with another activity • Denied again

If your answers mostly match below section, the function may be Automatic (Sensory)

Antecedent (Before Behavior)	Behavior (What Child Did)	Consequence (What Happened After)
• Quiet setting • Alone • Overstimulated • Boredom	• Hand flapping • Rocking • Repetitive noises • Spinning objects • Head banging	• No reaction • Redirected • Given fidget • Behavior continued

CHAPTER 11

Build an Effective Behavior Intervention Plan

BEHAVIOR INTERVENTION PLAN

A complete behavior intervention plan includes:

1. Antecedent Interventions
(Prevent the behavior before it starts)
2. Replacement Behaviors
(Teach the child what to do instead of the problem behavior)
3. Consequence Strategies
(How you respond after the behavior—either to reduce the unwanted behavior or increase the new skill)

Antecedent Interventions – Preventing the Problem Behavior Before It Happens

Antecedents are what happens right before a behavior. Antecedent strategies like adjusting the environment, offering choices, and using visual supports can help prevent challenging behaviors before they begin. These proactive steps make expectations clearer, help the child stay engaged, and support the use of appropriate behaviors. Simple changes can set the child up for success and make daily routines smoother.

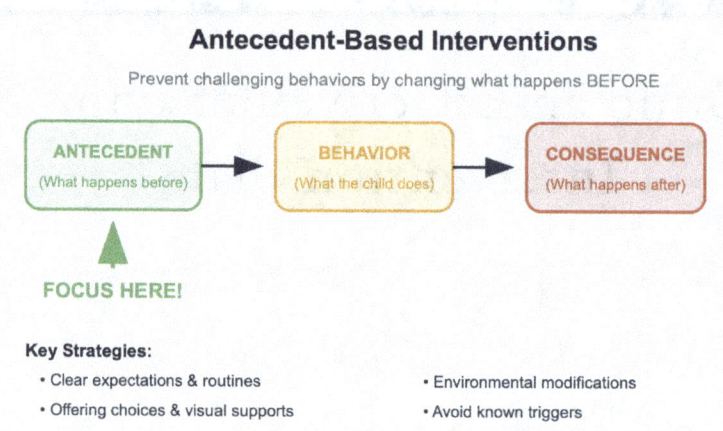

Image 1: Antecedent Based Intervention

Modify the Environment

- Make the space calmer, safer, and more comfortable so the child can stay focused.
- Remove harmful or breakable items from the area if the child throws things when upset.
- Tie back your hair if the child tends to put it in their mouth while playing.
- Set up a cozy quiet corner with cushions if the child gets overwhelmed easily, and ask him to take a break with soft music if they like.

Use Visual Supports

Visuals play a crucial role in supporting the child's understanding, particularly when verbal instructions alone may not be fully comprehended. They help prevent misunderstandings and provide a clear, consistent guide to what is expected.

- Help the child understand what to expect by using pictures or objects they can see.
- Use a picture schedule to show what happens first, next, and last (e.g., "First homework, then snack, then playtime").
- Show a visible timer to let the child know how much time is left before a transition.
- Offer a choice board with pictures of activities or snacks so the child has options to choose from.

Give Clear, Simple Instructions

- Make directions easier for the child to understand and follow.
- Use short sentences like "Put your shoes on" instead of long explanations.
- Avoid vague words like "Be good"—say exactly what you want them to do (e.g., "Sit on the chair").
- Use gestures, visuals, or show them what you mean if they're unsure.

Provide Warnings and Transition Cues

- Let the child know ahead of time that a change is coming so they can get ready.
- Give a "5-minute warning" before stopping a fun activity like TV or playing.
- Use a timer so the child can see how much time is left.
- Say what's coming next clearly: "In 2 minutes, we will clean up and go outside."
- Use a special song or phrase to signal a transition, like a cleanup song or "Time to move!"

Offer Choices

- Give the child some control by letting them choose between options you're comfortable with.
- Offer 2–3 simple choices (e.g., "Do you want apple slices or crackers?" or "Red shirt or blue shirt?").
- Use a choice board or visuals if the child has difficulty with spoken language.
- Allow them to choose the order of tasks when possible (e.g., "Do you want to do blocks first or books?").

Modify the Task (Demands)

- Make tasks easier to help the child feel successful and avoid frustration.
- Start small—if cleaning a whole room is too much, begin with "Put your toys in the bin."
- Give help at first, then slowly do less as the child learns the task.
- Adjust the task to match the child's current ability, and increase the challenge slowly over time.

Behavior Momentum

Behavior momentum is a strategy where you start by asking the child to do simple, easy tasks they can complete quickly and successfully. These early successes increase the likelihood that the child will comply with more difficult or less-preferred tasks that follow.

For e.g., first, ask the child to do a few simple actions like "clap your hands" or "touch your nose." Then, give a more challenging instruction such as "put away your toys." Because the child has already experienced success, they are more likely to cooperate with the harder request.

Use Noncontingent Reinforcement (NCR)

NCR is a strategy where reinforcement is given on a regular schedule. This helps meet the child's needs before they show any challenging behavior.

If the behavior serves to get your attention, provide attention on a regular schedule so the child won't feel deprived (e.g., spend 5 minutes playing or talking with the child every 30-minute interval).

Examples:

- Give access to favorite toys or activities on a set schedule (e.g., offering plush toys or music time), instead of only after the child requests in challenging ways.
- Provide affection, praise, or short breaks throughout the day so the child doesn't have to use big behaviors to "earn it."

***

Replacement Behaviors – Teaching Positive Behaviors as an Alternative to Problem Behavior

Replacement behaviors serve the same function as the problem behavior but are socially acceptable and effective. Challenging behaviors often occur because a child is trying to communicate a need, avoid an unpleasant or aversive situation, gain access to something desired, or satisfy a sensory need. Punishing or stopping the behavior alone does not teach effective communication or appropriate responses. Instead, replacement strategies teach alternative skills that help children meet their needs safely and positively. Learning these behaviors supports more appropriate interactions and reduces problem behaviors over time.

Know the Function Before You Teach a Replacement

Understanding why the child engages in a challenging behavior is essential. Are they trying to gain attention, escape a task, get access to a preferred item, or meet a sensory need? Identifying the function of the behavior helps you choose the right replacement skill—one that meets the same need in a safe and socially appropriate way.

Examples of Replacement Behaviors by Function

Attention-Seeking Behavior

If the child yells or interrupts to get attention, teach them how to appropriately gain it—such as using words to communicate. For example, if they want to play with you, they can say, "Can I play with you?" In other situations, they can say "Excuse me," raise their hand, or gently tap your arm.

Escape or Avoidance Behavior

If the child tries to avoid tasks by running away, dropping to the floor, or saying "no," teach them to ask for a break, say "help please," or use a break card or gesture to request assistance.

Tangible-Seeking Behavior

If the child grabs or demands toys, snacks, or electronics, teach them how to appropriately request items using words, sign language, or a communication device (e.g., "I want the ball").

Automatic (Sensory) Behavior

If the child engages in repetitive or self-stimulatory behavior for sensory input, offer safer alternatives that meet the same sensory need—like fidget toys, chewy necklaces, weighted items, or access to movement breaks.

Additional Guidance for Teaching Replacement Behaviors

1. Prompt, model, and support the child as they learn the new skill. Be ready to guide them through it until they can do it on their own.

2. Reinforce the replacement behavior immediately and consistently with praise, access to preferred items, or attention.
3. Be patient—learning takes time. Celebrate small successes along the way.
4. Gradually fade prompts to encourage independence.
5. Make sure everyone involved (parents, teachers, therapists) uses the same replacement strategy and reinforcement so the child learns faster through consistency.

* * *

Consequence Strategies – What to Do After the Behavior Happens

Before we talk about what parents should do after a behavior happens, it's important to first understand a key strategy used in ABA (Applied Behavior Analysis) called **Differential Reinforcement.** This means rewarding the positive behavior you want to see more often and not rewarding the challenging behavior. Over time, the child learns that using positive, appropriate behaviors helps them get what they want in a better way. Understanding this makes it easier to calmly and consistently respond when a problem behavior happens. Now that we know what differential reinforcement is, we can use it in different ways depending on the function of the child's behavior—whether they are looking for attention, trying to avoid a task, asking for a favorite toy, or meeting a sensory need.

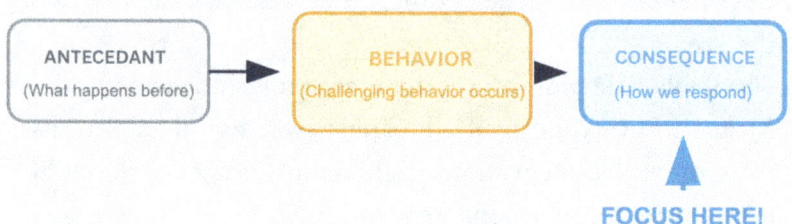

Image 2: Consequence Based Intervention

Attention-Seeking Behavior

Why It Happens
The child may want attention but doesn't yet know how to ask for it politely. Instead of using words like "Can you play with me?" they might yell, interrupt, throw things, or grab someone's arm to get noticed.

When the Challenging Behavior Occurs
Stay calm and neutral.

Don't react emotionally—no scolding, eye contact, or verbal correction.

Even telling them, "Stop yelling," gives attention and may accidentally reinforce the behavior.

Remember: attention—even negative attention—is still attention.

What to Do Instead
Teach Functional Communication
Model and teach the child how to ask for attention appropriately, such as:

- Teach "Excuse me."
- Teach gently tapping someone's arm.
- Teach the child to ask for play by saying 'play with me' or giving a picture card that says 'play with me'
- Teach using a speech-generating device to request, "Play with me."

Use Differential Reinforcement

Reinforce (reward) only when the child uses appropriate communication.

For example, if the child says, "Excuse me," stop what you're doing, make eye contact, and say warmly, "Thank you for asking so nicely! What do you need?"

On the other hand, if the child yells or grabs, do not give attention. Wait until they ask the right way—even if you need to prompt them—and then provide attention.

Increase the Reward for Independence:

If the child uses the skill without help, give even more attention—such as longer playtime, silly tickles, or a dance party. Say things like, "I love how you asked so nicely by yourself!" This teaches that polite, independent communication gets the best results.

Escape or Avoidance Behavior

Why It Happens

The child may try to avoid activities they don't like, such as brushing teeth, cleaning up, or doing homework. If they cannot ask for a break, they might cry, run away, throw things, or show other challenging behaviors.

When the Challenging Behavior Occurs

Don't remove the task right away. If you do, the child will learn that tantrums make tasks disappear. Stay calm and neutral—no angry voice, no big reactions. Some escape behaviors also seek attention, so avoid giving too much reaction.

What to Do Instead

Teach Functional Communication

Help the child ask for what they need in a respectful way:

- Teach "Break please."
- Teach "Help me."
- Teach "This is too hard."
- Teach showing an "All Done" card or a break card.

Use Differential Reinforcement

In the beginning, we teach the child to say "All done" (even if prompted). If the child uses this appropriately, we remove the task. If they do not use it, we keep the task in place.

Later, we teach the child to say "Break please" (even if prompted). If they ask appropriately, without showing challenging behaviors, we give a short break and then gently return them to the task.

We also teach the child to say "It's too hard" (even if prompted). When they do this appropriately, we make the task easier so it becomes manageable.

Another skill we teach is "Help please" (even if prompted). When the child asks for help appropriately, we provide assistance.

If the child shows any kind of challenging behavior, we do not remove the task or give a break. We wait for them to use the appropriate communication first, even if you had to prompt them, and then respond appropriately.

Increase the Reward for Independence

If the child asks for a break independently without challenging behavior, give the full reward (e.g., 10–15 minutes of iPad) and say: *"I like how you asked for a break all by yourself. Way to go!"*

If the child showed some challenging behavior first and then asked after prompting, give a smaller reward (e.g., 3–5 minutes of iPad), using a neutral tone:

"You earned this because I liked how you asked me for a break."

Access to Tangibles (Items or Activities)

Why It Happens
The child may want a favorite toy, snack, or game but doesn't yet know how to ask. They might scream, grab, or cry to get it.

When the Challenging Behavior Occurs
Do not give the item right after the problem behavior.
Giving in teaches them that tantrums work.
Stay calm and don't scold or argue in the moment.

What to Do Instead
Teach Functional Communication
Help them ask using:

- **Words: "I want cookie."**
- **Signs, pictures, or a speech device.**
- **Pointing to the item calmly.**

Use Differential Reinforcement
Give the item only when they ask appropriately.
If they first showed behavior but then (with your help) asked appropriately, give a small reward (e.g., 2 minutes of play).
If they ask independently without challenging behavior, give a bigger reward (e.g., 20 minutes of play) and lots of praise.

What If the Item Is Unavailable?
Offer alternatives kindly:
"That's not available right now, but you can choose this or that."

If behavior continues, wait for them to calm down and try again.

Sensory or Automatic Behavior

Why It Happens
Some behaviors—such as hand-flapping, rocking, or chewing—help the child feel calm or focused. These behaviors meet sensory needs, not social needs.

When the Challenging Behavior Occurs:
Safety first. If it's dangerous (e.g., head banging), protect the child.
Don't punish the behavior. It's often the only way the child knows to feel calm.

What to Do Instead
Offer Safe Sensory Alternatives:

- **Chewy necklaces**
- **Fidget toys**
- **Weighted blankets**
- **Bouncing balls**
- **Hand massages or deep pressure**

Teach Functional Communication

- Teach "I want squeezes."
- Teach "Quiet time, please."
- Teach pointing to a sensory item or using a communication device.

Use Differential Reinforcement
Praise the child when they use a safe sensory item:
"I like how you're using your chewy!"
"Great job using your sensory box."

If the child engages in unsafe behavior, calmly redirect:
"Let's use your sensory box instead."
"We use the heavy blanket like this."
Keep your voice calm and body language gentle

Other Helpful Strategy: Differential Reinforcement of Incompatible Behavior (DRI)

<u>What is DRI?</u>
Teach the child to do something that cannot happen at the same time as the problem behavior.

<u>Examples:</u>
If the child bites their nails, teach them to keep their hands in their pockets or fold their arms.

If the child sniffs their hand after touching private parts, offer a pleasant-smelling object or lotion to smell instead.

If the child plays with saliva, redirect them to water play with bubbles to meet the sensory need.

CHAPTER 12

Phases of Challenging Behavior

THE STAGES OF BEHAVIOR CHANGE: FROM PROBLEM BEHAVIOR TO POSITIVE COMMUNICATION

Understanding the child's behavior can feel confusing—especially when you're trying to change challenging behaviors. ABA (Applied Behavior Analysis) gives us helpful tools and concepts to make things clearer.

Three important terms to know are: extinction, extinction burst, and spontaneous recovery.

These words describe what often happens when you stop reinforcing (rewarding) problem behavior

What is Extinction?

Extinction means you stop giving attention or rewards to a behavior that used to work for the child. When that behavior no longer gives them what they want, it starts to go away.

<u>Example:</u>
The child screams to get candy.

In the past, you may have given them the candy just to avoid a meltdown.

So they learned:

"If I scream, I get candy."

Now you use extinction.

When they scream, you stay calm and don't give the candy.

You wait for them to calm down and ask nicely, like "I want candy."

Over time, they learn:

"Screaming doesn't work anymore. I get candy if I use my words."

They begin to make the connection that:

Screaming = no candy

Asking nicely = candy

This makes the screaming behavior start to fade away.

What is an Extinction Burst?

When you first stop rewarding or reinforcing problem behavior—like giving candy when the child screams—they may scream louder, cry harder, or throw a bigger tantrum at first. This is called an extinction burst. It's like they're saying: "Hey! This always worked before! Let me try HARDER!"

<u>Example:</u>

You used to give candy when the child screamed. Now you don't. Suddenly, they scream louder, throw themselves on the floor, or cry longer. That's the extinction burst. It's normal and expected.

<u>What should you do at that time?</u>

Stay calm. Stay strong. If you don't give in, they'll learn that even BIGGER behavior doesn't work. Then the behavior will start to go away.

But if you give in during the burst, they'll learn: "Oh! I just have to scream more, and I still get what I want!" So next time, the behavior may get even stronger.

What is Spontaneous Recovery?

After the behavior has stopped for a while, it might suddenly happen again. That's called spontaneous recovery. It doesn't mean you did anything wrong. It's just the child testing: "Hmm... will screaming work again today?"

<u>Example:</u>

The child hasn't screamed for candy in two weeks. Then one day—boom! They scream again. Don't worry. It's just a quick test. Just stay calm and don't give the candy. The behavior usually disappears again very quickly if you don't reinforce or reward it. When you use extinction, you're teaching the child a powerful lesson: "Only calm and appropriate behavior gets me what I want." It may take time and patience—but it works!

BACK MATTER

I hope parents will find this book helpful and encouraging as they support their child's growth and development. While there are many more components that could be explored, I have focused on the most essential ones to provide a clear and approachable guide without overwhelming families. Alongside skill-building strategies, I have written about how we approach and manage challenging behaviors that may limit a child's ability to learn and fully engage with the world around them. These behaviors are addressed thoughtfully and respectfully, always keeping the child's well-being at the center. My intention is to empower parents with practical tools and insights they can use in everyday life. I understand that every child is unique, and I hope this book serves as a meaningful step toward building confidence and clarity in their journey.

References

Association for Science in Autism Treatment. (n.d.). Applied behavior analysis: A treatment summary. https://asatonline.org/for-parents/learn-more-about-specific-treatments/applied-behavior-analysis-aba/

Behavior Analysis in Practice. (2018). The effectiveness of applied behavior analytic interventions for children with autism spectrum disorder. *Behavior Analysis in Practice, 11*(2), 123–135. https://doi.org/10.1007/s40617-018-0025-6ScienceDirect

Cooper, J. O., Heron, T. E., & Heward, W. L. (2020). *Applied behavior analysis* (3rd ed.). Pearson.

Journal of Applied Behavior Analysis. (2020). Long-term effects of applied behavior analysis interventions on children with autism. *Journal of Applied Behavior Analysis, 53*(4), 789–802. https://doi.org/10.1002/jaba.727

Miltenberger, R. G. (2016). *Behavior modification: Principles and procedures* (6th ed.). Cengage Learning.

Alberto, P. A., & Troutman, A. C. (2019). *Applied behavior analysis for teachers* (10th ed.). Pearson.

Leaf, R., & McEachin, J. (1999). *A work in progress: Behavior management strategies and a curriculum for intensive behavioral treatment of autism*. DRL Books.

Maurice, C., Green, G., & Luce, S. C. (1996). *Behavioral intervention for young children with autism: A manual for parents and professionals*. Pro-Ed.

Tarbox, J., & Tarbox, C. (2017). *Training manual for behavior technicians working with individuals with autism*. Academic Press.

Koegel, L. K., & Koegel, R. L. (2006). *Pivotal response treatments for autism: Communication, social, & academic development*. Paul H. Brookes Publishing.

Schreibman, L. (2005). *The science and fiction of autism*. Harvard University Press.

Matson, J. L., & Sturmey, P. (Eds.). (2011). *International handbook of autism and pervasive developmental disorders*. Springer.

Hanley, G. P. (2021). *Practical functional assessment and skill-based treatment: Enhancing quality of life for individuals with autism or intellectual disabilities*. Context Press.

Carr, E. G., Dunlap, G., Horner, R. H., Koegel, R. L., Turnbull, A. P., Sailor, W., ... & Fox, L. (2002). Positive behavior support: Evolution of an applied science. *Journal of Positive Behavior Interventions*, 4(1), 4–16. https://doi.org/10.1177/109830070200400102

REFERENCES

Bailey, J. S., & Burch, M. R. (2022). *Ethics for behavior analysts* (4th ed.). Routledge.

Miller, J. S., & Singh, N. N. (2023). *Cultural humility in behavior analysis*. Springer.

Bearss, K., Johnson, C., Smith, T., Lecavalier, L., Swiezy, N., Aman, M., ... & Scahill, L. (2015). Effect of parent training vs parent education on behavioral problems in children with autism spectrum disorder: A randomized clinical trial. *JAMA*, 313(15), 1524–1533. https://doi.org/10.1001/jama.2015.3150

Lucyshyn, J. M., Dunlap, G., & Albin, R. W. (2002). *Families and positive behavior support: Addressing problem behavior in family contexts*. Paul H. Brookes Publishing.

Schächinger Tenés, R., Lieb, A. H., & Meyer, A. H. (2025). A meta-analysis of applied behavior analysis-based interventions to improve communication, adaptive, and cognitive skills in children with autism spectrum disorder. *Journal of Autism and Developmental Disorders*, 55(3), 1234–1248. https://doi.org/10.1007/s40489-025-00506-0SpringerLink+1

National Institute of Child Health and Human Development. (2019). Early intervention for autism. Eunice Kennedy Shriver National Institute of Child Health and Human Development. https://www.nichd.nih.gov/health/topics/autism/condition-info/treatments/early-interventionNICHD+1

Bhawna Aggarwal (Sonia) is a Board Certified Behavior Analyst (BCBA), International Behavior Analyst (IBA), and a licensed behavior analyst in Texas and North Carolina. She is also licensed in Ontario, Canada, as a Registered Behavior Analyst. With over six years of clinical experience, Sonia specializes in working with autistic children and their families across diverse settings, including homes, clinics, and schools.

Sonia holds a Master of Science in Psychology and Applied Behavior Analysis from Eastern Kentucky University and a specialization certificate in Autism and Behavioural Science from Mohawk College. Her expertise spans comprehensive behavioral assessments (e.g., ABLLS, VB-MAPP, ESDM, PEAK), functional behavior assessments, and the development of individualized intervention plans.

Passionate about parent education and advocacy, Sonia is dedicated to making ABA principles accessible and actionable for families. She has presented at professional conferences and regularly trains caregivers on behavior strategies and parenting supports. Sonia is particularly known for her compassionate, evidence-based approach, and her use of innovative methodologies such as Skill-Based Treatment (SBT) and Project ImPACT to promote positive outcomes in children with autism.

Bhawna Aggarwal (Sonia)
M.S (Psych.), BCBA, IBA, LBA (TX, NC), RBA (ON)
Email: get2soniabcba@gmail.com
LinkedIn: https://www.linkedin.com/in/basonia/
Educational Blogs: get2sonia.medium.com

www.ingramcontent.com/pod-product-compliance
Lightning Source LLC
Chambersburg PA
CBHW050329010526
44119CB00050B/729